HOW TO MAKE JEWELRY OUT OF ANYTHING

A Complete Out-of-the-Box Jewelry Making Guide for Teens and Teens-at-Heart!

42 quirky jewelry-making ideas that are full of life and originality, including six projects to help you learn the craft from scratch

momsandcrafters.com

Copyright © 2018 Menucha Citron
All Rights Reserved.

No part of this book may be reproduced, transmitted, or stored by any means or in any form except for your own personal use, without express written permission from the author. Author can be contacted at menucha@momsandcrafters.com

ISBN: 978-0-9980794-4-8

Visit momsandcrafters.com for craft tutorials, free printable crafts and coloring pages, and to learn more about the author.

CONTENTS:

GETTING STARTED — Page 5	**WHY MAKE JEWELRY** — Page 6	**BASIC SUPPLIES** — Page 10	**6 TO LEARN** — Page 15
FOCUS: FINISHES — Page 22	**4 WITH GLITTER** — Page 23	**4 WITH NAIL POLISH** — Page 28	**4 WITH PAINT** — Page 33
FOCUS: WHERE YOU FIND YOUR MATERIALS — Page 38	**4 WITH NATURE** — Page 39	**4 WITH GARBAGE** — Page 44	**4 WITH CRAFT BASICS** — Page 49
FOCUS: THINKING DIFFERENTLY — Page 54	**4 BEADS GONE AWRY** — Page 55	**4 COOL FRIENDSHIPS** — Page 60	**4 WITH PAPER** — Page 65

- Supplies resources - Page 70
- Project Index - Page 71
- About the Author - Page 72

PROJECT GALLERY:

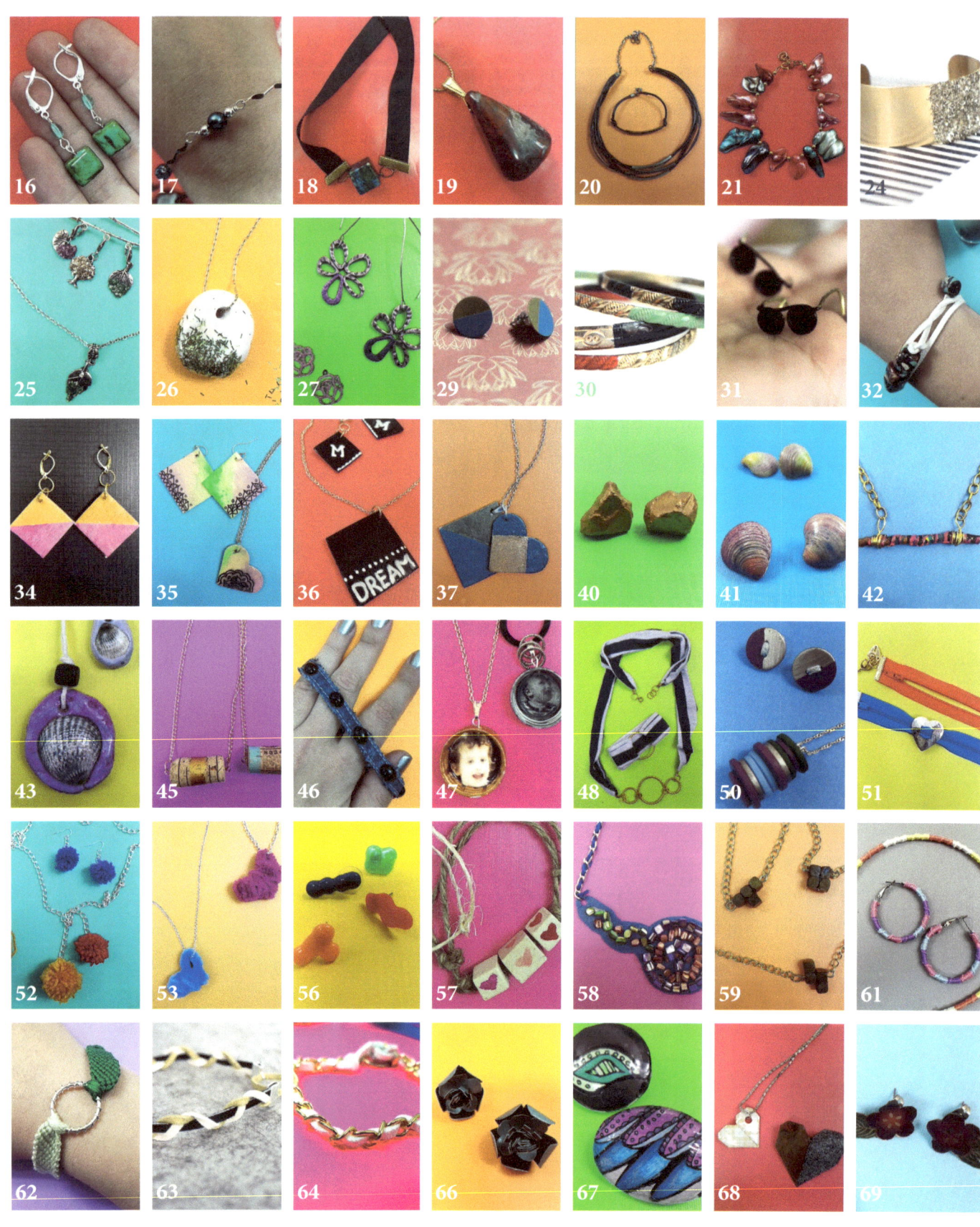

GETTING STARTED

The main thing that's stopping you from moving forward? That first step. Take the plunge with the projects in this section. They will equip you with the knowledge that you need to get started.

WHY MAKE JEWELRY OUT OF ANYTHING?

My story:

I like to make jewelry. Duh. But how did I come to love it so much? Back when I was a moody, suffering teen some seventy years ago - just kidding - more like fifteen, I started to craft. I spent endless hours making scrapbook pages with my high school photos.

But I honestly didn't have a budget. I ended up using only paper and found items, which sounds awesome, except that I found myself cutting out tiny letters by hand, traced from computer printouts. I lost all my patience.

Then, my baby sister inspired me. She took her bat mitzvah money, bought jewelry making supplies, and overnight recouped the twenty dollars by selling her creations to friends.

I had always dreamed of buying the entire jewelry-making aisle but it was too expensive. When I saw what my sister did, I realized I can do it too. And so started twelve years of jewelry-making bliss.

Jewelry making was therapeutic for me. I'd sit and create my pieces for hours, deep in my own thoughts. I brought it with me wherever I went. And I still do it to this day.

One thing that has changed, though, was my approach. I used to stick to the jewelry-making aisle. Now? Not so much.

Breaking the rules - legit!

Some rules are meant for keeping. Some were designed to be broken. Never break the law. Always break self-imposed societal norms surrounding the intended use of craft supplies.

Maybe I was just dying to break some rules and this was a safe way to do it? Whatever it is, I do know that I like to use things for things other than their intended purposes.

A huge focus of this book, as you'll see, is using out-of-the-box materials as

well as found ones. Did you ever think that NAIL POLISH would get a dedicated storage container in your tiny craft room?

Nail polish makes the best jewelry paint if you ask me...

And when it comes to budget-friendly crafting, both nature and the recycling bin are your best friends. One of my favorite pieces of jewelry is my gold-nugget earrings.

Gold nuggets, huh?

They're actually painted rocks. I literally wear rocks on my ears and everyone says to me "Those earrings are amazing, where'd you get them?"

My reply: "I painted some rocks..."

I have no shame.

While some of these jewelry-making tutorials break the rules on materials, some focus on new ways to do things with the same materials. For example, check out pages 55-59 for new ways to use beads - melting them, gluing them together, writing on them...

I also share some ways to turn classic friendship-bracelet type jewelry into something totally glamorous and unique. It's a bit of a random chapter, but I LOVE it because it features some of my old-time-classic favorite pieces.

Be you, because you're awesome:

There's no one quite like you out there, which is why there is one rule that I ALWAYS follow when it comes to jewelry making - or any type of craft:

Make it your own.

When I design these crafts, I always try to include some way to switch it up. In some crafts it's easier to find, in others, you have to be creative.

Use these as springboards to make your OWN thing. For example, where I share pom-pom jewelry ideas, you can make a double dangle earring with two mini pom-poms. I share the general concept and how I did it. Stick on some googly eyes if you want something totally crazy...

I have included some "Make it Yours" tips along the way, but don't stop there!

You're not perfect, I'm not perfect, let's all be imperfect together:

There's one thing that can destroy the joy of crafting: perfectionism.
I love seeing an end-result when I craft.
It doesn't have to be a perfect end result. It has to be pretty. It has to be functional. (Yep, I do like functional stuff - maybe that's another reason I ditched scrapbooking for jewelry making?)

But expecting things to be perfect is unrealistic because we are humans and not machines. Imperfection is beautiful - it adds that handmade quirkiness that is so unique.

Join me in embracing the imperfections as we craft, and in creating beautiful handmade jewelry together.

Oh, the things that you'll learn!

No, this is not meant to be a "teach yourself how to make jewelry" book. It's more in the league of "craft inspiration for your crafting club/summer camp/winter break."
You'll find some great gift ideas too that you can make for your friends.

However, I don't take for granted that anyone reading this knows how to make jewelry, and some projects *do* require basic skills - such as opening and closing jump rings, making loops, and more.

That's why I include a section with basic techniques and tools you'll need to get started. Bonus: that means more projects!

I also include some info on supplies that you never imagined you'd be making jewelry with... zippers, anyone?

Some skills may require help.
While these crafts were designed for anyone ages 10-110, some require things like poking a hole into a thin piece of wood. You may want to check in with a parent for help with these.

I include a note for those that require adult supervision for a small part of the task, however I always make sure that the AWESOME parts of the craft can be done by anyone!

Credit where credit is due:

I won't pretend to have been able to do this alone...

I want to extend a huge thank you to Plaid Crafts for helping, not only by sending me some amazing FolkArt and Martha Stewart Crafts paints and Mod Podge products to help me figure stuff out, but also by providing endless inspiration in sending their stuff.

I want to thank my entire blogging tribe and friends, as well as my blog readers and newsletter subscribers who answered all my questions, provided insight and inspiration, joined my focus group to help me figure out the technicalities of this book, and supported me endlessly.

I want to thank Alyssa, of the Arts & Crackers blog, for always being my partner in the sisterhood of crazy crafters (come join our group on Facebook!)

I want to thank my parents who always encouraged my hobbies and outlets, my mom for proofreading this book, and my siblings who always embraced my craziness. I especially want to thank my baby sis, Shoshana, who inspired me to start making jewelry to begin with.

I want to thank Baby Y for not totally destroying all the projects I designed for this, for kindly agreeing to eat snack after snack while I photographed, and for not toppling my lighting equipment.

I want to thank my big boy, M, for being patient with me while I crafted, for allowing me to craft without him repainting everything, and for "agreeing" delightfully to eat pizza and pasta for dinner while I got stuff done.

Most of all, I need to thank my dear husband, Shmuel, not only for believing in me, but for encouraging me, serving as a sounding board for my frustrations, bathing the kids, doing the dishes, embracing my nuttiness, telling me I can do it, and everything else he does day in and day out that made this book actually happen.

Thank you!
Happy Crafting!
Menucha (Citron) Ceder
momsandcrafters.com
craftwithanything.com

BASIC SUPPLIES FOR JEWELRY MAKING

Granted, if you want to connect an earring to something that is meant to be an earring, you'll need earrings, right?

Here are the basic supplies you'll want if you plan to make any jewelry - even awesome jewelry. It's not an all-encompassing list. You'll learn more about supplies as you go along, as you follow different tutorials, and as you shop for them. These are the ones you'll need for this book and some other basic projects.

1. Tools: You don't need anything fancy. Just get a basic starter set of pliers - a round nose, chain OR needle nose, and wire cutter (Image A).

Needle nose pliers have slightly narrower jaws than chain nose pliers, but both will serve the same purpose. I recommend getting one with a serrated jaw (a jagged one) to start with (B). It can mark your metal but it grips it more easily. Unless you're working with fine metals, you should be good with it.

2. Findings: Findings are all the little links that will connect your pieces and turn them into jewelry. Some basics you'll need for the projects in this group:
- The parts that turn it into a specific piece. For example, earring pieces for earrings (C) Flat pad earrings can be glued to various items (D).
- Clasps for your necklaces and bracelets - there are many types of these too (E).
- Things like pin-backs if you're making a pin (F). To make a pendant you can use a pendant bail (G).
- The connectors/ "building blocks". Jumprings are those little rings that you can open and close (H). Headpins are little wire sticks with tiny "nail heads" at the end that block a bead from falling off and that can be closed with a little loop (I). Eyepins have a loop at the end (J) but you can make your own (page 16). Crimps and crimp covers are "squashed" against a string to secure it (K-L)
- Another favorite for these out-of-the-box crafts are ribbon crimps (M). These are end pieces that can be

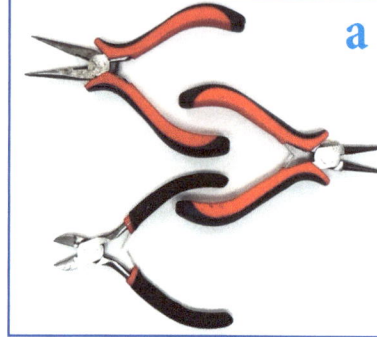
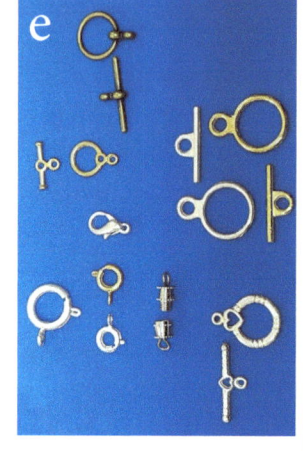
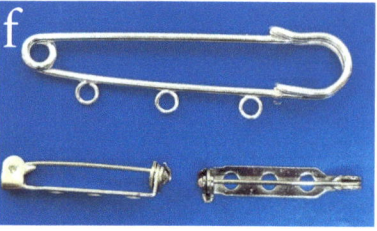
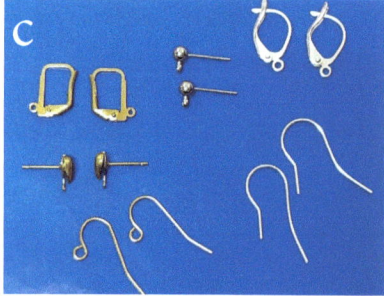
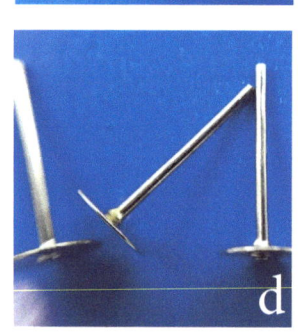
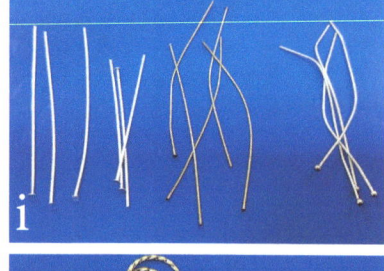
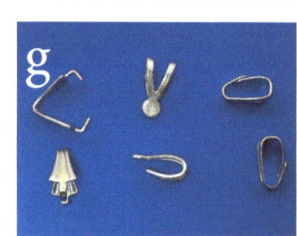
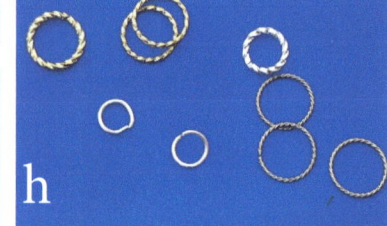
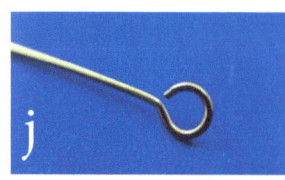

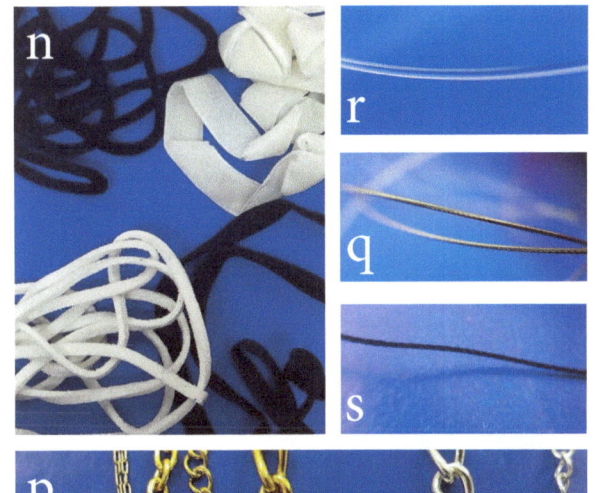

clamped down on ribbon to connect them to other findings. Cord ends are similar and used to finish off a narrower cord. There are many other "finishing bits" that you can use, and each one comes in many different styles.

3. The stringy things: Ribbons, chain, cord, wire - have it all! The more crafty and non-jewelry-like your projects are, the more you'll want cords and ribbons (N). You can get leather cord (fake is cheaper), silk or satin cord, regular satin ribbon, or whatever you want!

Wires (O) are a favorite - more about that later!

Chains also come in many types (P). You'll want to use them both for connecting parts, and as chains for pendants. You can purchase finished chains, ready with clasps, for your pendants.

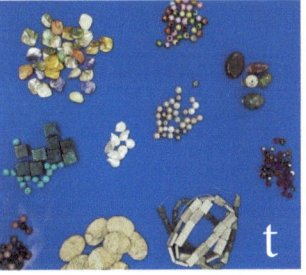

For beading, I use thin wire or string. My favorite, tigertail (Q), is made up of tiny wire strands twisted together and coated with nylon. Fishing line is fun to use for an invisible effect (R). Stringing thread is also a great option (S).

4. Beads, charms, and more: Surprise, surprise! Most of these projects do *not* use beads! But a few do. And so, I need to elaborate.
Better quality beads (T) tend to come in glass, metal, or natural materials (such as gemstones or pearls).

I love wooden beads (U) because they typically have larger holes for stringing on to thicker materials and because they're CHEAP!

I use metal beads (V) - usually small ones - to add a bit of a "real" touch to the project. If you feel like your crafts need that extra touch, metal beads, charms, links, and bead caps (W-X) are perfect for that. You can see how I added a heart slider to one of my zipper bracelets (page 51) and a charm duo to the other to make them feel more like jewelry.

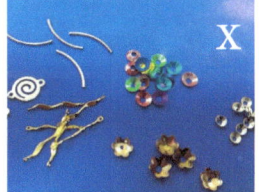

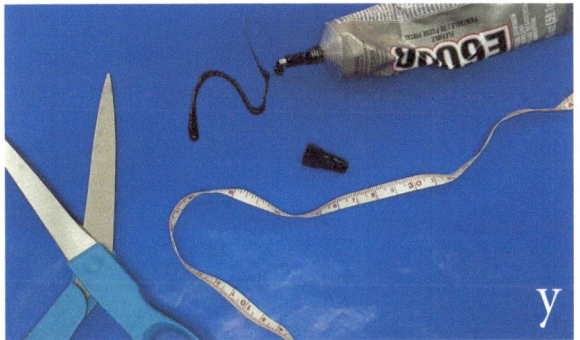

5. The kitchen sink: Obviously I don't mean that literally. But there are many odd bits and pieces that you'll also want to have in your stash (Y):
- Glues: I like E6000 glue for almost anything, but sometimes I use super glue, wood glue, or anything that's created for a specific material that I'm using. E6000 is my favorite because it can glue smooth surfaces, such as metal and glass,

11

together. Most glues will only connect porous surfaces, such as paper and wood. When a specific glue is needed in this book, I specify.
- Ruler: I use this sometimes when I feel like things should be even. I should probably use it a little more.
- Scissors: you'll want these handy to cut stuff other than wire. I don't think I need to elaborate.

Know your sizing:

Most beads are measured in millimeters (mm). You probably won't need to measure each one. As you create your pieces, you'll start learning more about sizes and you'll be able to understand it without seeing the bead.
- Smaller beads are 2-6mm
- Average is 8-10mm
- Large would be 12-16mm

And then you have larger statement beads in any size upward of that, into the twenties and even thirties. Keep in mind that 10mm=1cm, so if you know your centimeters, that's where it'll start getting more comfortable for you.

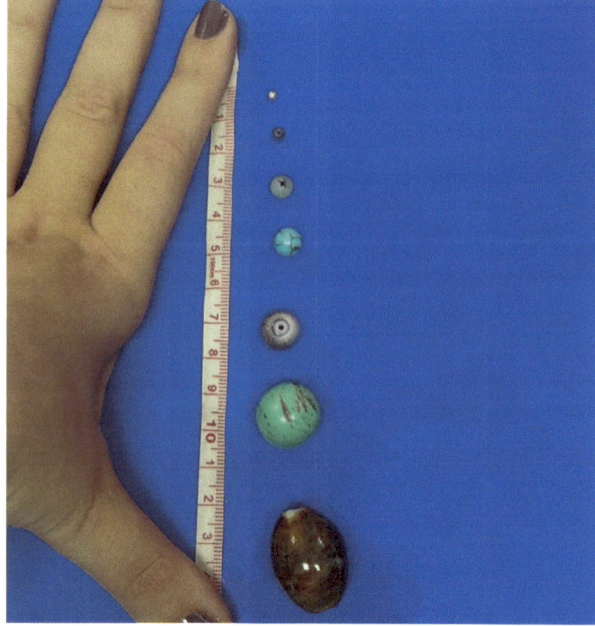

Most findings are also measured in millimeters.

Wires, on the other hand, are measured in gauge. It's tricky, though. The larger the gauge, the thinner the wire.

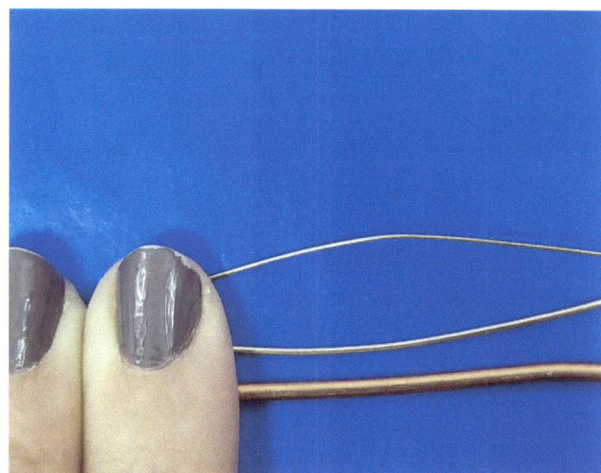

- 28 gauge wire is very thin and will hardly hold its shape, making it perfect for wire crochet or threading beads.
- 24 guage is slightly thicker and easier to work with, but also doesn't hold its shape well. If you try to make eyepins with these, you'll need to make twisted loops (page 17) instead of simple ones (page 16).
- 20 gauge wire is possibly the one I use the most. It won't fit into the holes of all beads (such as pearls and some gemstones) but it's very sturdy and holds its shape, so when I can I use it.
- 14-16 gauge is very thick and you'll probably need special pliers to get anywhere with it (unless it's made from something soft, like sterling silver.) I've used this, and even 12 gauge wire to make bangles. You probably don't want to touch this until you have more experience working with metals. It's not for basic jewelry crafts.

In a nutshell: to build your basic jewelry making stash, I recommend having both 24 and 20 gauge wires handy.

Pay attention to the final size of your piece too, especially with bracelets. Most bracelets that come with measurements in this book are for an average seven-inch size.

What it's made of:

You can get your findings in any type of material, but I recommend choosing gold- or silver-tone metals - or both.

Once you see what you like, you can get more colors and even splurge on some sterling silver or gold-filled pieces.

Keep in mind that precious metals are much softer than non-precious ones, so you'll need to be more careful and use pliers without serrated jaws, or even nylon jaws.

You CAN get plated metals if you want it to feel real but the thin plating can sometimes flake when you're working with it.

For sensitive ears, I recommend either getting earring pieces only in metals that work for you, or using surgical steel (which is cost-effective AND gentle.)

BASIC SUPPLIES FOR THESE UNIQUE PIECES

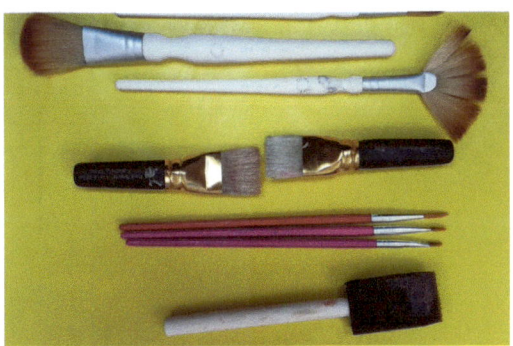

Many of the chapters focus on a specific material and so I have included some brief materials tips on those in their respective chapters.

However, there are some basics that you'll need across the board that wouldn't fit into the regular jewelry-making categories. Yep, I'm about to outline for you a basic craft stash - but that's what this is about! Bring jewelry making into your regular crafts for a cool, functional end-result.

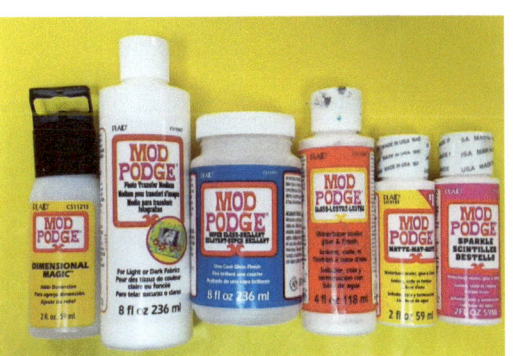

Mod Podge:

This wonder material comes in many different formulations. For jewelry, I recommend using Mod Podge Super Gloss. It's a thicker formulation that dries less sticky than the original.
You can also use Mod Podge Dimensional Magic to add a hard, thick coat on top.

Wood Pieces:

I use many wood shapes, especially in the "Paint Finishes" section (Page 33). That chapter elaborates more on the paints I use, but the wood pieces are pretty cool because they serve as a blank canvas in a material that's easy to wear.

I use thin wooden pieces that are lightweight. They DON'T have holes. I use a craft knife to poke holes and it's a bit awkward (and should be done by a grown-up!) Another alternative would be an awl. Or just buy it with holes to begin with!!

Clay:

I use clay in a couple of projects. The reason I didn't include this with the regular jewelry-making supplies is because I don't always use the typical polymer clay that most people make jewelry with!!

The clay I like to use is an air-dry clay that's meant for kids. It works great in pendants! You can leave it natural, paint it afterwards, or color it with richly-pigmented water-based paints before you work with it.

I added a shiny coat of polymer-clay glaze to make it look sophisticated. On some of them, I add different cool finishes that I press in.

Markers and such:

Chalk markers, permanent markers, paint markers, whatever it is - you definitely want to have these in your stash!

I have a large pack of permanent markers in every color, as well as a chalk marker that I use for touching up stencil work. I also have some paint markers, which are perfect for writing on dark-colored beads.

At the end of the day, this book will have been successful if *you* manage to add to this list, if *you* find *your* jewelry-crafting style and if *you* learn how to think outside the box to make something totally unexpected.

Find the courage to deviate and experiment. Don't be afraid to fail - you can simply try again.
Enjoy the process and be flexible with the results.

For additional video demos and resources to help you with the projects in this book, visit craftwithanything.com.

SIX TO LEARN

Use these simple tutorials to learn the basics of jewelry making for beginners. These don't fall into the "unconventional" category; but I figured, instead of just showing you how to do the stuff, why not make a functional piece out of it? Make each of these a few times, changing up the styles, until you master the skills! These projects are so basic that the "pretty factor" will be determined by your choice of materials.

SIMPLE LOOP EARRINGS

This basic loop will be the building block of your jewelry from now on! A simple drop-earring is the perfect learning project, but try making linked necklaces and bracelets using this skill!

You'll also learn: Connecting earrings to earwires and findings to finish them off.

SUPPLIES:
- 2 headpins
- 2 eyepins (or make your own - see FYI below)
- 2 earwires
- 2 larger beads and 2 coordinating smaller beads

TOOLS:
- round-nose pliers
- chain-nose pliers
- wire cutters

INSTRUCTIONS:
1. String your main bead onto a headpin (Image A).
2. Trim it using your wire cutters, leaving a "tail" of about 8mm (Image B).
3. Use your chain-nose pliers to fold the tail end of your headpin to the right, at about a 90-degree angle (Image C).
4. Starting from the tip of your wire, use your round-nose pliers to roll it into a loop (Image D). You'll need to "squash" it completely closed using another pair of pliers, but you will do that after you attach it to the link you're about to make.
5. Place a smaller accent bead onto an eyepin. Repeat steps 2-4 to complete a beaded link (Image E).
6. Attach your link to your first beaded dangle by linking the loops together and then, using a pliers, squashing the open loop closed to form a complete loop (Image F).
7. Most earring findings have a loop that opens. If yours does, use your pliers to open the loop. ALWAYS OPEN LOOPS with a forward/backward motion - twisting the circle to move the ends apart, not widening the hole - this weakens the loop. (Image G). If your earwire doesn't have a loop, open the beaded link you created and attach it to the earwire instead. You just made a pair of earrings!!

a

b

c

d

e

f

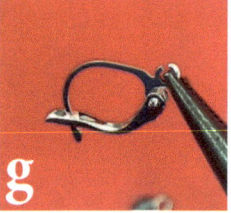
g

FYI To make your own eyepin, simply take a bit of wire and create a loop at the end, just like you did in this tutorial!

WRAPPED LOOP BRACELET

Sometimes the hole of a bead is too small to fit a-22 gauge or thicker headpin, and you need to use a thinner one that won't hold its shape. Wrapping loops is another way to keep them secure!

You'll also learn: How to finish off bracelets and necklaces with clasps. Using a few chain links as your clasp connector makes it adjustable - how cool?

SUPPLIES:
- 24-gauge wire
- 6-8mm beads
- links
- spacer beads
- clasp and a few links of thin-link cable chain as a connector

TOOLS:
- round-nose pliers
- chain-nose pliers
- wire cutters

FYI If your clasp or chain is fixed closed and doesn't open, just create your wrapped loop around it to begin with.

INSTRUCTIONS:

To make this link bracelet, you'll be making a lot of beaded links and connecting them with metal links. But since you can't open a wrapped loop, you need to connect them as you go along. These instructions should be repeated for the entire length of the bracelet.

1. Take a small piece of wire, a few inches long, and fold over, starting 1 cm from the end, using your round-nosed pliers (Image A). Create a curve, not a sharp fold.
2. Cross the short end of the wire over the long part, and thread on a link (Image B.)
3. Close your loop, keeping the link intact (Image C). To close a loop, grip the curve you created in step 1 with one pair of pliers and use the other pliers to wrap the short end of the wire around the longer part (Image G). When you're done, use the wire cutters if necessary to trim the leftover bit of wire. Press it against the coil you created using pliers (Image H).
4. Add a bead. Spacer beads can also be added to give it a more polished look but are totally optional! You can also use bead caps here (Image D).
5. Trim, leaving about 1.5 cm from the end and fold it over as you did in step 1 (Image E). Insert another link and finish off your wrapped loop around the link as you did in step 3 (Image F).
6. Continue with your bracelet making a pretty pattern until desired length is reached (Images G-H).
7. To finish off your bracelet, attach a clasp to one end and a few links of chain to the other. To open your clasp and chain, find where it opens and grip it on each side with pliers, opening in a forward/backward motion and NOT pulling it apart because that would weaken it (Image I).

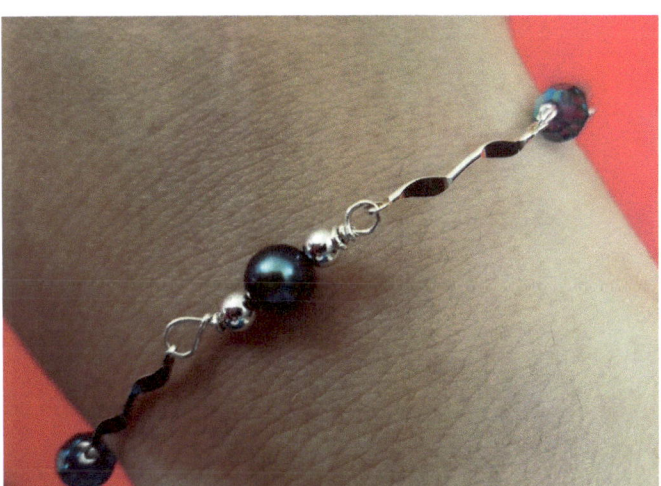
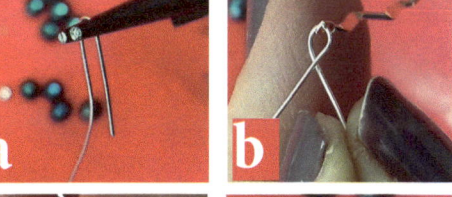
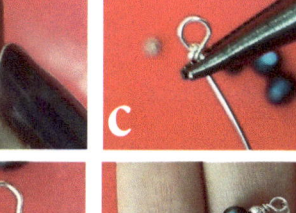
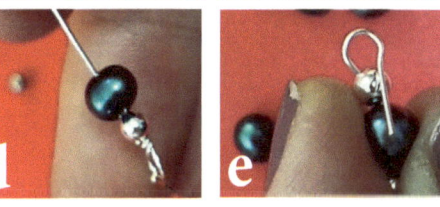

RIBBON CRIMP CHOKER

Ribbons can be used in so many ways in jewelry making - the key is to finish it off properly so that you have a polished result. Ribbon crimps are essential; make sure to get a size that works for your project.

You'll also learn: How to properly open and close and use jumprings.

SUPPLIES:

- one focal bead
- one eyepin (or make your own - see FYI on page 16)
- about 1 foot of ribbon
- 4 ribbon crimps that match your ribbon size
- clasp
- 5 jumprings

TOOLS:

- round-nose pliers
- chain-nose pliers
- wire cutters

INSTRUCTIONS:

1. Place your focal bead on your eye pin and make a simple loop flush against the bead (Image A). If you forgot how to do this, refer to page 16, steps 3 and 4.
2. Open two jumprings using a back and forth motion - not pulling them apart (Image B.) Attach them to the loops on each side of your bead (Image C).
3. Figure out how long you want your choker to be and cut two ribbons that will add up to the desired length minus an inch. Attach a ribbon crimp by placing the end of a ribbon inside and squeezing it firmly shut using the chain-nose pliers (Image D) so that it holds in place and passes the "tug test" - see FYI on this page. Do this to each end of each ribbon. (Image E).
4. Connect one ribbon to each jumpring that you attached in step 2.
5. At the other end of one ribbon, attach three jumprings to make your necklace adjustable (Image F). To the other end end of the other ribbon, attach a clasp.

FYI Make it strong! Do the "tug test. A great way to avoid losing a piece of jewelry because you didn't make it strong enough is to give three firm tugs on it when you're done connecting the parts. This way you can see if it will hold up to normal wear and tear.

a

b

c

d

e

f

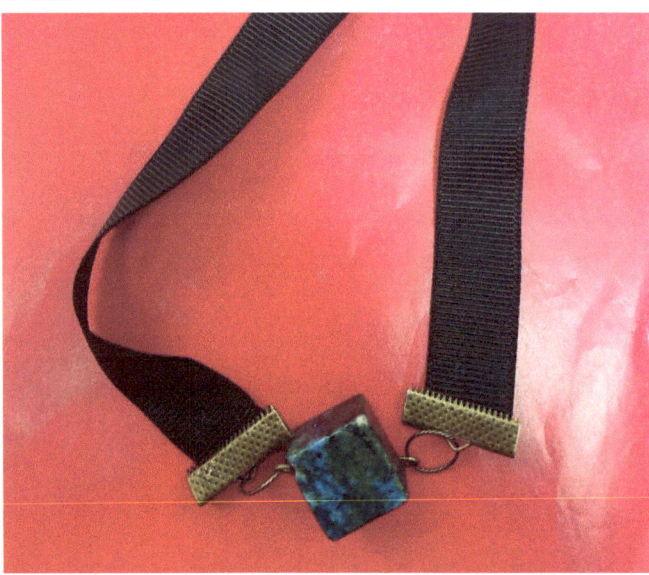

SKILL I have already mentioned two ways to close a clasp:
1. Connect it to a few jumprings
2. Connect it to a few links of chain.

If you don't want it to be adjustable, you can use a single jumpring or purchase connectors designed for this purpose. For the sake of keeping things simple, from now on, I will simply write "clasp and connector" instead of specifying WHICH connector, and you can choose your preferred one!

PENDANT BAILS PENDANT

Almost anything with a hole drilled near the top can be turned into a pendant with the right type of bail. Attaching a bail is simple! There are SO many types of pendant bails and each one has a special use, but in this book you'll mostly find yourself using a snap-on bail. Another convenent bail to have handy is an ice pick bail - it helps to convert an object that doesn't have an existing loop on top into a pendant.

SUPPLIES:
- one focal bead with a hole drilled towards the top.
- one ice-pick bail
- one snap-on bail
- one jumpring if needed
- a finished chain

TOOLS:
- any two pliers

INSTRUCTIONS:
1. Widen the opening of your ice pick bail with your fingers so that it fits over your focal bead.
2. Place it onto your focal piece so that the prongs enter the hole and press it closed with your fingers (Image A).
3. If your focal piece was drilled from front to back rather than side to side, you'll need to use a jumpring to make it hang the right way. Use your pliers to open your jumpring and insert it into the top of the ice pick bail. I did not need to do that on this pendant.
4. Snap on your snap-on bail by pressing the jumpring if used, or the ice pick bail into the opening.
5. Snap or slide the snap-on bail onto your finished chain and wear your necklace with pride.

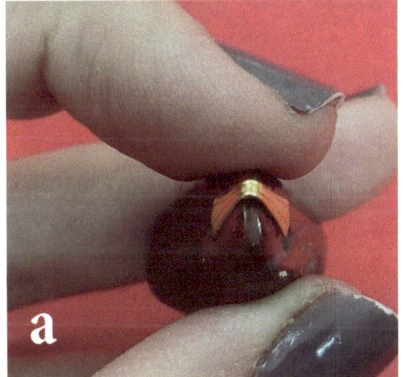
a

SKILL This project was a bit more complicated than necessary to highlight two types of bails. Any bead placed on a headpin with a loop on top can be converted into a pendant with a snap-on bail added!

CORD ENDS SET

Whether you're using cord as a central focus of your jewelry or you're just using it for a pendant chain, finish it off properly with a clasp and wear it many times over.

SUPPLIES:

- 9-10 feet thin leatherette cord
- 5 curved metal tube beads with holes large enough to fit your cord twice.
- 4 cord ends (2 thin, 2 wide)
- a few inches of chain
- 2 sets of clasp and connector

TOOLS:

- any 2 pliers

INSTRUCTIONS:

1. **Bracelet:** Cut two pieces of cord about 8 inches long.
2. Thread them together through a tube bead.
3. Knot your cord at each end of the bead to keep it in place. I allowed for a little space for it to move around.
4. Measure your bracelet size, and trim your cords to about 1-2 cm. smaller than you want your finished bracelet to be.
5. Place the two cords from one side into the cord end so that the loop faces away from the rest of the string (Image A). Hold it with one pair of pliers and use the other to fold down one side of the crimp (Image B). Make sure your string is still properly positioned and fold down the other side. Do the tug test (see FYI on page 18). Repeat this step for the other end of the bracelet.
6. Attach your clasp and connector to the loops on your cord ends (Image C).
7. **Necklace:** Cut eight 1 foot lengths of cord. Thread them in pairs through four metal tube beads (Image D).
8. Now, take all 8 strands (4 pairs) of each end and repeat step 5. This will be much more challenging with more cords! The trick is to have the right size cord ends for your project.
9. Attach a length of chain to each side to complete your desired necklace length. Finish off with a clasp and connector.

FYI Cord ends are made to fit around a single cord, but if you use a larger size with a thinner cord, you can fit multiple strands like I did here.

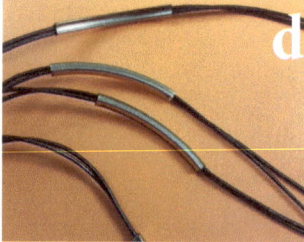

CRIMP BEAD BRACELET

These little beads literally crimp down on a wire, cord, chain, or whatever and hold them in place. Here, I will teach you a very basic stringing technique that I love to use with statement beads.

SUPPLIES:

- about 6 inches worth of your favorite beads and spacer beads
- 2 crimp beads
- optional: 2 crimp covers
- about 8 inches of tigertail wire (it's easier to work with a longer wire so if you can, trim it when you're done)
- clasp and connector

TOOLS:

- 2 pliers, one should be chain nose
- wire cutters

INSTRUCTIONS:

1. Slide a crimp bead about 1 inch into your tigertail, followed by a clasp (Image A). Slide the end of your wire back into the crimp bead from the direction that it exited (Image B.)
2. Use your chain nose pliers to gently move the crimp bead up closer to the clasp - allowing just enough space for the clasp to move around freely. Squash it closed (Image C).
3. Add a crimp cover if using over your bead; squash it closed (Image D)
4. Thread on your favorite beads. If your bead hole is large enough, thread your first beads over the tail of the tigertail wire from the first 2 steps. Otherwise, trim it close to the crimp (Image E).
5. When your bracelet is about 1 inch shorter than you want it (Image F), add a crimp bead and connector, and thread the tigertail back into the crimp bead just like you did in step 1 (Image G). Thread it through the last few beads if the holes are large enough.
6. Finish off your bracelet like you did in steps 2 and 3 and trim your tigertail wire (Image G).

SKILL Crimps come as beads or tubes. They are interchangeable but each has its advantages. Beads look more polished if your crimp will show. Tubes are easier to work with if you're using regular pliers. Crimping pliers are available but not necessary. Crimp covers are also optional, but they DO help reinforce your crimp and make it stronger AND they add a very polished look.

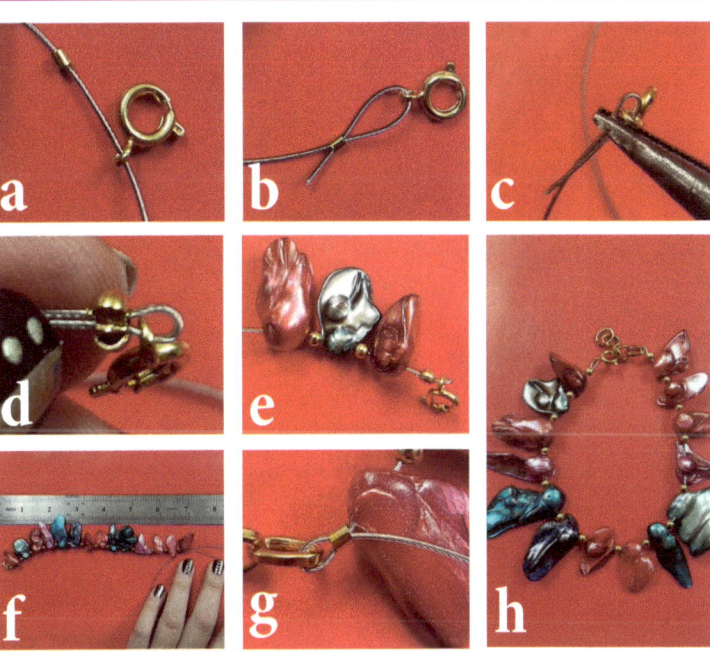

BE INSPIRED BY THE FINISH

From glitter to nail polish, be creative with the finish of your jewelry and go crazy creating and crafting!

FOUR WITH GLITTER

Glitter can add sparkle to anything - even jewelry! There are different types of glitter. I like to use glass glitter because it's more substantial, can be pressed into clay more easily, and feels more "real" on jewelry. Tinsel glitter comes with more variety, but it's super light and thin - and it's made from plastics. Make sure that you always finish off your glitter jewelry project with a layer of sealer or decoupage so that it doesn't shed!

GLITTER BLOCKED CUFF

Color block may be sharp, but how about glitter block? This cuff starts with a base that you buy, but you can also use this tecnique to spruce up some old jewelry! I love the deceptive simplicity of this project!

SUPPLIES:

- a blank metal cuff base
- glass glitter
- Mod Podge
- a foam brush
- a plate or paper to catch the glitter

FYI Crushed glass glitter is better for the environment. It also gives it a luxe look and is less likely to shed - although the Mod Podge helps too. Try it on stamping blanks with a hole on top and turn them into dangle earrings

INSTRUCTIONS:

1. Paint a thick, but not drippy, layer of Mod Podge on a small area of your cuff.
2. Holding it in one hand over a paper plate, gently shake on a single layer of glitter. Don't try spreading or pressing it on once it's on the cuff - it'll make a big mess. Allow it to dry completely.
3. If you'd like better coverage, once it's dry, dab on a bit more Mod Podge with your finger. Shake on another layer of glitter. Allow it to dry completely.
4. When you're satisfied, dab on some more Mod Podge with your brush, but use your finger to make sure it's spread evenly. The final look is so high end - but *you* know how simple it is to make!

LEAF CHARMS

Glitter is a totally unique way to add a touch of color to an otherwise-ready piece. I don't even remember where these leaf charms came from, but here's a perfect way to upgrade anything that needs a bit of life!

SUPPLIES:
- charms that can use a bit of color
- Mod Podge
- crushed Glass Glitter
- pin or pendant bail and finished chain.

INSTRUCTIONS:
1. Apply a thick layer of Mod Podge to the area you'd like to color. Use a cotton swab to clean up anywhere you DON'T want glitter.
2. Add a generous amount of glitter, one color at a time.
3. Allow it to dry completely.
4. Finish with a final layer of Mod Podge. Allow it to dry completely.
5. Attach your charms to a pin or to a pendant bail and chain.

SKILL

Just from reading the introduction, you have the skills needed to finish your own chain. Want the step by step? First, cut a piece of chain to size. Then, attach a jump ring to each end. Attach a clasp to one end. To the other, attach something to clip your clasp onto. Some options are: a few jump rings, a tab with a hole meant for this purpose, or twisted cable chain - just a few links to make it adjustable. Whatever you use, make sure your clasp fits through it comfortably. You can also buy a ready-made finished chain, or swap with chains from your other jewelry.

CLAY PENDANT

Take your glitter-blocking up a notch by making the base for it from scratch! Make a clay base, then press in some glitter. I used tinsel glitter on this one, but glass glitter would work even better.

SUPPLIES:
- air dry clay
- tinsel glitter
- clay glaze
- paint brush
- Mod Podge
- chain or cord, finished (see FYI below)

TOOLS:
- optional: clay-shaping tools. If you don't have these, have a toothpick handy.

INSTRUCTIONS:
1. Carve a piece of clay for your pendant into any creative shape, using tools if you'd like.
2. Poke a hole using an appropriate clay-shaping tool or toothpick. Allow it to air dry completely.
3. Brush a bit of Mod Podge where you'd like the glitter to be. Sprinkle on glitter. Allow it to dry completely.
4. Paint a layer of clay glaze on top and allow it to dry completely.
5. Remove the clasp and thread the chain through the hole. Replace the clasp.

NOTE:
When I first made this, I tried applying the glitter directly to the wet clay. Because it's tinsel glitter, it just doesn't stick. If you're using glass glitter, you'll be able to press it in while it's wet, as I did with one of the seashell necklaces on page 43.

FYI "Finished" chain or cord means that it has the clasps attached and is ready to be used for a necklace, whether purchased or DIY.

SKILL For this project, I used air-dry clay because I didn't want to bake the plastic glitter. Most jewelry projects use polymer clay which needs to be baked to harden fully.

PETAL EARRINGS

I love collecting unique pieces to use in projects like this. For these earrings, I used both common filigree roses and flowers that were hand-picked in a bead shop. The different colored earrings are so quirky!

SUPPLIES:
- flower components or drops
- very fine glitter
- Mod Podge
- a thin paint brush
- 6 inches of 18 or 20 gauge wire or ready-made earwires

TOOLS:
- round nose pliers
- chain nose pliers (for this project non-serrated is best).
- wire cutters
- a metal file if making your own earwires

INSTRUCTIONS:
1. Apply Mod Podge to one of your petals or on the entire piece.
2. Pour an even layer of glitter over it. Allow it to dry completely.
3. Attach an earwire. For this project I made my own earwires - and you can too - see the "SKILL" box.

SKILL
Make your own earwires! First, make sure your wire is totally straight. Next, use your chain nose pliers to bend it just before the midway point and form the back into a curve (Image A). Then, form a loop on the bottom using your round-nose pliers (Image B). Tip: use a file to make the end that goes into the ear less rough. Make your second one using the same measurements.

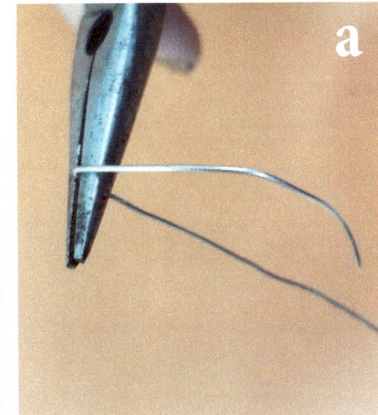 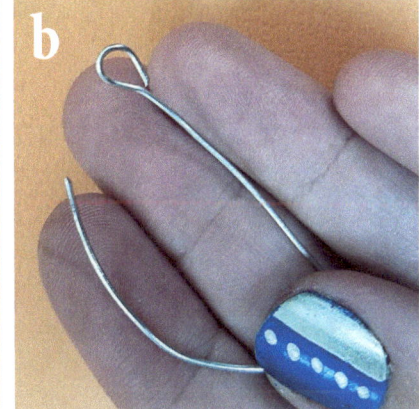

a b

FOUR WITH NAIL POLISH

I LOVE using nail polish in all sorts of crafts - it's a great way to use the colors that didn't really work out and to incorporate unique textures in my projects. I supplement my discards collection with dollar store nail polish, including a top coat, of course. I have every color in the rainbow among my craft supplies - and you're about to see why! So why nail polish and not paint? First of all, it's so EASY to use! It has the brush built in, and is meant for fine work. It's also surprisingly durable, and you can easily remove it and start again by using... nail polish remover!

COLOR BLOCKED STUDS

I color blocked these earrings, but you don't need to. Attaching a metal blank to ear studs gives you a blank canvas to paint *any* design with nail polish - be creative!

SUPPLIES:

- stamping blanks (metal discs that are meant for stamping)
- nail polish
- flat pad ear studs
- earring backs if your studs don't come with them.
- E6000 glue

INSTRUCTIONS:

1. First, design your stamping blank however you'd like! For these color-blocked studs, I simply swiped the nail polish brush horizontally at the point I wanted the color to end and painted in the rest. Allow it to dry completely.
2. Follow with a top coat of nail polish.
3. Glue your stamping blanks onto your studs. Be aware of the placement of the studs - you probably want them towards the top of the blanks, not dead center, especially if your stamping blanks are large. Allow them to dry completely before wearing.

UNTIRED BANGLES

Giving tired old jewelry a facelift is a super cool way to update your wardrobe. It's quick and so much fun, and open-ended enough to totally unwind and relax with. Try it on other jewelry too!

SUPPLIES:

- old bangles (or get cheap fashion-jewelry bangles)
- nail polish - the more colors the better!

INSTRUCTIONS:

1. Paint your bangles with nail polish. I played with different patterns, as pictured. On some I did small stripes, one got painted half way, and one got wider blocks of varnish. The cool thing about nail polish is that it's easy to be precise with it - you don't need to use painter's tape. Just paint.
2. Add a second layer of polish if you want, allow it to dry, and finish with a top coat. Allow it to dry completely before wearing.

MAKE IT YOURS

Try this on hoop earrings or any old jewelry! Try using a glitter topcoat - the main point is to take my idea, experiment, and go wild with it!

SUNGLASSES CHARMS

One of my favorite crafts ever, these sunglasses charms show how versatile nail polish can be! Make a few to hang on a charm bracelet or wear it as a delicate and surprising pendant.

SUPPLIES:
- a few inches 20 gauge wire
- dark nail polish (the color you'd wear your sunglasses)
- finished chain or lobster claw clasp.
- optional: wood glue

TOOLS:
- chain nose pliers
- wire cutters
- round nose pliers

INSTRUCTIONS:
1. Form two loops in the center of your wire (Image A). Make them small so the nail polish will spread properly (mine are about 8mm.)
2. Bend back the wires to form the sides using your chain nose pliers (Image B).
3. Use the round nose pliers to form the end of one arm into an arc (the part that would go around your ear). Form a loop at the end of the second arm. Trim. (Image C).
4. Grip your glasses in your weak hand. Sweep some nail polish across the "lenses" of the glasses (Image D). The trick to getting this part right is loading the brush just enough so that it will pool in the holes and not drip. If you're having trouble, you can first dip the glasses into wood glue, allow it to dry, and then paint with nail polish, but I skipped this step. Allow nail polish to dry before continuing, propping it upright while it dries.
5. Attach a lobster-claw clasp to the loop you formed in Step 3 to make a charm, or string a finished chain through that hole.

a

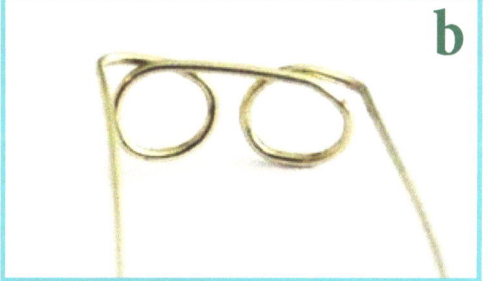

b

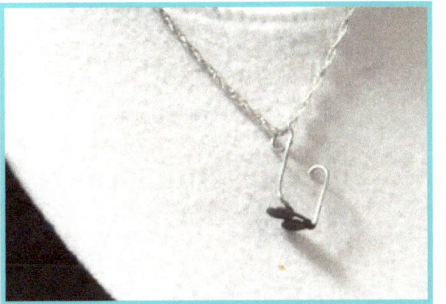

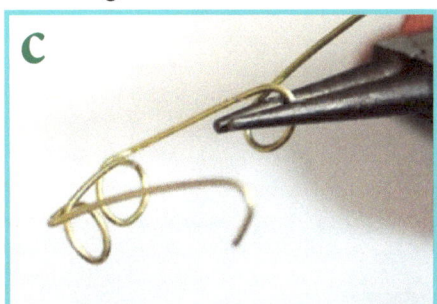

c

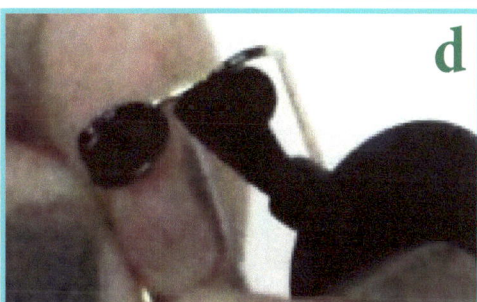

d

MARBLED "GEMS"

Not every bracelet needs to close with a clasp! This wrap bracelet has ends that tuck in and it's surprisingly secure - and easy to put on yourself.

SUPPLIES:

- wooden beads (you need a total of 5 dipped beads for this project)
- nail polish in a few colors
- a bowl with water
- cord
- a chenille stem/pipe cleaner
- E6000 glue
- a baby wipe or wet paper towel

INSTRUCTIONS:

1. Thread a few wooden beads on a chenille stem (the fuzziness holds it in place). Bend up the ends so that you can grip it easily.
2. In a bowl with water, drizzle a few drops each of two to three colors of nail polish (more colors will make it look muddy).
3. Dip your beads into the nail polish, pulling up the polish so the beads get coated (Image A). Place on a moist paper towel or baby wipe to dry.
4. When it's dry, cut a piece of leather cord that fits 3.5 times around your wrist.
5. String on 3 beads and knot on each end to hold them in place (Image B).
6. Dab a dot of glue on both ends of your cord, and attach another bead to each end, stringing the cord so that it stops halfway through the bead. Flood the hole of the bead with extra glue. Allow it to dry completely.
7. To wear this bracelet, just wrap it around your wrist and tuck the end beads under the cord to hold it in place (Image C).

FYI Use natural colors for a more "gemstone" feel. Look at photos of your favorite stones and choose colors from there.

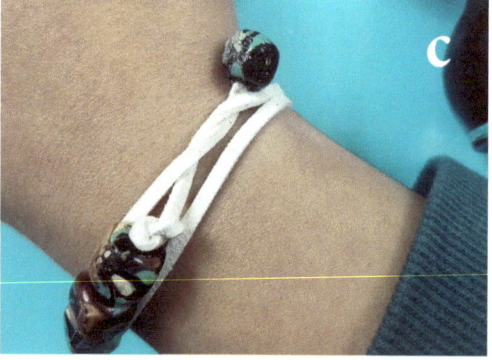

FOUR WITH PAINT

Paints come not only in unique colors - they come in amazing textures too! In this chapter, I show you how to use paint to create luxurious looking textures on basic materials. All of these are painted on flat wooden shapes (my "blank canvas") but you can also paint beads, cardboard - the choice is yours! Brushes matter! For watercolor, I recommend a soft-bristled brush, or a brush with its own water tank called a "water brush". For the finishes, such as concrete, I recommend a coarse brush for texture. For brushed metals, regular acrylics, and other non-specific paints, a foam brush gives you even coverage, while finer brushes will help you add detail and clean up your work.

BRUSHED METAL

Brushed metal is one of my favorite textures - and one that's so natural in jewelry! But incorporating it in unexpected places adds a unique twist while maintaining a classy but energetic vibe!

SUPPLIES:

- wooden shapes: a square and a triangle that fits half the square.
- FolkArt Brushed Metal paint
- Martha Stewart Crafts Soft Gel Watercolors
- 2-4 pretty jumprings
- earwires
- wood glue (E6000, glue gun, or even tacky glue will work too)

TOOLS:

- an awl or craft knife
- a watercolor paint brush
- two pliers of any type

INSTRUCTIONS:

1. Using an awl or craft knife, poke a hole at one corner of your square - an adult's job (Image A).
2. Paint the squares with brushed metal paint.
3. Paint the triangle with a bright, bold watercolor. If you'd like, dilute the watercolors to allow wood texture to show through.
4. Once they're all dry, glue the triangles on top of the squares with two sides lined up.
5. Attach one jumpring through the hole in the wood. Attach a second one if needed - depending on the direction of the hole in your earwire - you want the decorative sides to face forward.
6. Attach your earwires and wear with pride!

a

MAKE IT YOURS

Make more holes and dangle beads from the bottom. Try it with different shapes, textures, and colors. The possibilities are endless!

WATERCOLOR DOODLES

I love watercolors. I love doodles. Why not combine them into a fun jewelry set? The watercolor paints are natural on the wood and the inexpensive supplies allow trial and error for your doodles.

SUPPLIES:
- wooden shapes
- jumprings
- Martha Stewart Crafts Soft Gel Watercolors
- thin permanent marker
- earwires
- finished chain
- clear nail polish

TOOLS:
- an awl or craft knife
- two pliers of any type
- paintbrushes

INSTRUCTIONS:
1. Use an awl or craft knife to poke a hole at a top corner of your wooden shapes - an adult's job.
2. Paint your shapes using watercolors. Try experimenting with no more than two colors at once.
3. Once it's dry, play with doodles! If you'd like, you can pencil them in first. Then trace with permanent marker (Image A).
4. Seal with clear nail polish. Allow to dry.
5. Attach a jumpring (two if necessary) to connect to earwires or chain.

FYI Clear nail - what? You saw in the previous chapter that nail polish is great for color. So why not as a sealer? Usually I use clay or decoupage sealers; but here, the decoupage, which would have made sense, caused my doodles to smudge (see the necklace design). The nail polish didn't (see the earrings.) Clear nail polish is also great for protecting plated metals and coated beads (such as fake pearls) to keep them from rubbing out for a bit longer.

SKILL Scared to draw your own design? Trace one by rubbing the back of a printed pattern with pencil. Place it over your wooden piece, and use a pen to trace the design, pressing hard. You can then trace the transferred pattern with a marker.

a

CHALK IT UP

If you love the look of chalkboard, this funky jewelry set is spot-on! Leave it unsealed so you can switch up the design, or seal it with clear nail polish if you plan to keep it as is.

SUPPLIES:

- wooden shapes
- FolkArt chalkboard paint
- chalk marker
- FolkArt erasable liquid chalk and lettering stencils (optional)
- jumprings
- earwires or finished chain
- clear nail polish (optional)

TOOLS

- paint brush
- awl or craft knife
- any two pliers

INSTRUCTIONS:

1. Poke a hole at a top corner of your wooden shapes - an adult's job.
2. Paint your shapes with chalkboard paint (Image A). Allow it to dry completely.
3. Add designs! You can use the liquid chalk and stencil or a chalk marker (Image B). If you stencil your lettering, due to the small sizes, you'll probably need to "clean it up" with chalk marker. Allow it to dry.
4. If you want, you can seal it with clear nail polish. Allow it to dry.
5. Attach your jumprings and earwires or chain and enjoy!

a

b

CONCRETE METALLIC

One of the coolest perks of paint finishes is the ability to mix cool textures that you wouldn't otherwise be able to get without real skills. I made these as a single necklace - but you can make earrings too!

SUPPLIES:

- wooden shapes
- FolkArt Painted Finishes concrete paint
- FolkArt brushed metallic paint
- jumprings
- finished chain

TOOLS:

- paint brushes - coarse ones like FolkArt Shortie brushes and a fine one too.
- awl or craft knife
- any two pliers

INSTRUCTIONS:

1. Poke a hole at a top corner of your wooden shapes - an adult's job.
2. Paint a blocked off section using your brushed metallic paint. Allow it to dry.
3. Paint the rest of it using the concrete paint. Use a fine brush for the edges next to the metallic (Image A); dab the rest on using a coarse brush. Allow it to dry.
4. Attach your jumprings and chains and wear it with pride!

a

MAKE IT YOURS

Take this project and run away with it! Concrete beads are normally heavy. Paint plastic beads with concrete finish; they'll be lightweight and SO cool! Try different textured paints: moss on wood, rust on metal - the possibilites are endless if you experiement.

BE INSPIRED BY WHERE YOU FIND YOUR MATERIALS

Nature? The recycling bin? Where it's from doesn't matter. Just go with it!

FOUR WITH NATURE

Craft materials found in nature are as free as it gets - and they add a crunchy, organic feel to your jewelry. Don't have one where you live but still like the project? You can purchase most of these in craft stores! I've highlighted three materials in this book: rocks, twigs, and seashells, but there are many more! See what you can make with acorns, leaves, seeds, and whatever else you find and love.

GOLD NUGGET EARRINGS

These are possibly my favorite earrings, if for no other reason, because of people's reactions when they compliment me. When they tell me how cool they are, my response is "Thanks. They're rocks." Own it.

SUPPLIES:

- small rocks - look for rough-surfaced ones, not smooth ones.
- FolkArt metallic paint in gold
- a paintbrush
- flat pad ear studs
- earring backs - rocks are heavy, so go for the type with the plastic discs attached.
- E6000 glue

INSTRUCTIONS:

1. Paint your rocks all over with the brushed gold paint. Allow them to dry completely.
2. Glue your rocks onto your studs. Be aware of the placement of the stud - make sure they will sit where you want them to. Allow them to dry completely before wearing.

FYI Heavy studs need extra support. Earring backs (or earnuts) with those plastic backs are usually referred to as "comfort clutch" backs and help these stay where you want them without pulling on your ears.

MERMAID EARRINGS

These are insanely simple, yet they're so exciting and unique! You can also make a matching necklace by coloring the shells in the project on page 43 following the instructions on this page.

SUPPLIES:
- small-ish seashells in pairs of similar size and shape
- craft watercolors, diluted
- clear nail polish or glossy Mod Podge
- flat pad earring studs and backs
- E6000 glue
- a paintbrush

INSTRUCTIONS:
1. Wash and dry your seashells well.
2. Paint a thin wash of your favorite colors. Tip: work with the natural pattern of the shell when switching colors.
3. When it's completely dry, coat with a protective layer of glossy Mod Podge or a nail polish top coat.
4. Glue a flat pad earstud to the back, making sure to place it so that it will sit nicely on your ear. Allow it to dry completely before wearing.

TWIG NECKLACES

Turning a real stick into a necklace is totally cool! And it looks classy too. This necklace will wear down with lots of use, but the nail polish coating on the twig will ensure you get lots of enjoyment out of it first.

SUPPLIES:
- a twig, approximately 2 inches long
- old nail polish
- a varnish coat (I used clear nail polish)
- 20 gauge wire
- chain - either a finished chain, or unfinished chain + a clasp + some jumprings or cable chain

TOOLS:
- wire cutter
- chain nose pliers
- round nose pliers

INSTRUCTIONS:
1. Clean off your twig really well and trim it neatly. Let it dry completely
2. Place it on a protected surface and drizzle different colors of nail polish. Let it dry completely.
3. Apply a protective coat of clear nail polish; allow it to dry completely.
4. Start wrapping your wire about a centimeter from one end of your twig (Image A).
5. Twist the end into a loop and finish wrapping it so that it looks pretty. I wrapped about 8 times, but use your own judgement (Image B).
6. Repeat on the other side and tuck your wire ends into the wrapping so that no sharp edges show.
7. Add a chain and you're done!

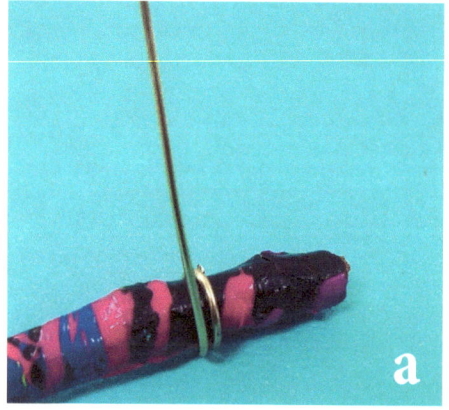

a

b

FYI Adding a touch of metal to something otherwise colorful turns it into a sophistiacated-yet-quirky piece!

SKILL Check that out! You just learned how to wire wrap! Now that you know the basics, try another wire wrapping project.

SEASIDE NECKLACES

This project is a step up from the glitter clay pendants I shared with you earlier. Not only are seashells added, but I teach you how to color the clay and a new unique texture you can add.

SUPPLIES:
- white air dry clay
- water based paint (I used gouache)
- small seashells
- glass glitter and/or chalk pastels
- scissors
- a toothpick (or anything long and thin to poke a hole)
- cotton twine or other string
- wooden beads
- clay glaze
- paintbrush

INSTRUCTIONS:
1. Color your clay by mixing in some gouache. Note: this is messy so protect your hands and surface!
2. Shape it into your desired shape and press in a shell. Poke a hole near the top and fix your shape if needed.
3. Press in textures (optional). Use glass glitter or you can use scissors to shave chalk pastel and press the shavings in. Allow it to dry completely.
4. Paint with a coat of glaze and allow it to dry. Make sure your hole still goes through.
5. String a piece of twine (or ribbon, or anything really) through the hole. Add a bead if you want, knot in place if you like how knots look. Make it long enough to slip over your neck.

NOTE:
Because of the casual style of this necklace, I just tied it closed. If you prefer, use cord ends, pliers, jumprings and clasps to finish this off as you would a ribbon (see page 20).

FYI
Air dry clay can be brittle. Follow package instructions to make sure your clay is thick enough and won't crack. Usually, it needs to be 1/4 inch thick to be strong.

FOUR WITH TRASH

Yes, I did say "trash." I feature four materials here: corks, t-shirts, bottle caps, and old jeans. But you can dig a little deeper and take it further. Try metal bottle caps, discarded flatware, old plastic toys - just use your imagination and see what you can create! While you may not have all of these available as garbage, you can ask others for help with getting them, or purchase them from craft supply stores. Even if you buy the materials, you are still getting your inspiraton from unique places.

CORK NECKLACES

The markings on these cork necklaces add so much character. You can ask a grown-up for corks, or purchase them at a craft store.

SUPPLIES:

- a cork.
- 2 eyepins - or make your own with 20 gauge wire.
- 2 jumprings - use pretty ones if you can!
- chain
- clasp
- chain or jumprings to connect to clasp.
- nail polish or metallic paint and brush
- E6000 glue

TOOLS:

- wire cutters
- round nose pliers
- chain nose pliers

INSTRUCTIONS:

1. Paint accents on your corks if you'd like, and allow them to dry.
2. Poke a hole in each end using your eye pins. It takes a bit of force so just do as deep as you can - at least 6mm.
3. Trim the stick of the eyepins to the depth of your holes. Dip them in glue and place them in the holes. Allow to dry completely.
4. Attach two pieces of chain to the eyepins using jumprings.
5. Finish your chain with a clasp and a connector.

SKILL In this project, we made a full necklace rather than a pendant by connecting something on two sides with chain. You can apply this to many other projects.

FYI In this project as well as in many of the projects in the "Paint" chapter, the jumprings are very visible. Why not add some interest and use the readily available pretty twisted ones?
You can also use screw eyes instead of the eyepins - it'll be easier - but they're not as elegant.

JEANS BRACELET

These are as casual as it gets - but don't have to be. Hint: the more metal you add, the less casual they'll look. I used the seams of the jeans to take advantage of the stitched detail.

SUPPLIES:
- old denim clothing
- ribbon crimps
- clasp and something to connect it to
- fabric scissors
- clear nail polish
- things to decorate with.

TOOLS
- chain nose pliers and a second pair of pliers - any type

INSTRUCTIONS:
1. Choose a nice part of the denim and cut a strip long enough to fit your wrist snugly.
2. Seal the rough ends with clear nail polish to prevent fraying.
3. Attach ribbon crimps to the ends.
4. Attach clasp and connector to the ribbon crimps.
5. Add your decorations - be creative with this!

MAKE IT YOURS
This project is really easy to make your own because it's all in the decorations! Some ideas:
- Sew on chain. Hang charms if you want.
- Glue on cabochons (flat back, undrilled stones) like I did using E6000.
- Paint it!
- Glue on rhinestones and gems.
- Sew on butttons.
- Embroider it.

FYI
Here's another great use for nail polish: stop edges from fraying! This works on ribbons, cords, fabric, and many other applications. If you do actually want the edges to fray, you can skip step 2 - as long as your stitches are intact like mine.

BOTTLE CAP PHOTOS

What a unique way to preserve a favorite photo! These necklaces would look much cooler on metal bottle caps, but when you're crafting from the trash you work with what you've got!

SUPPLIES:
- a bottle cap
- printed photo small enough to fit inside
- headpin
- pendant bail
- finished chain or cord.
- optional: decorative beads or jumprings.
- Mod Podge Dimensional Magic
- paint if you're using plastic caps.
- glue

TOOLS:
- awl or craft knife
- round nose pliers
- you may want another set of pliers to help you along

INSTRUCTIONS:
1. Paint your bottle cap - if you want to - before starting. Allow it to dry.
2. Trace the bottle cap on your image and cut the photo slightly smaller than the cap. Glue it in place inside your cap.
3. Coat the photo inside the cap with Mod Podge Dimensional Magic, allowing it to pool in a thin layer. Allow it to dry completely.
4. Use an awl or craft knife to poke a hole in the top of the cap - adults only. (Image A).
5. Poke your headpin through the hole from the inside to the outside, trim (Image B), and create a simple loop.
6. Attach a pendant bail and a chain or cord. If you'd like you can add beads or jump rings to the cord like I did.

OLD TEE JEWELRY

When creating fashion jewelry, you can think of it as an accessory. This upcycled t-shirt jewelry set shows you just how cool that can look.

SUPPLIES:
- an old t-shirt with a pretty print
- ribbon or cord ends (for the necklace)
- large circular links or components
- jumprings (for the necklace)
- clasp (for the necklace)
- needle and thread (for the bracelet)

TOOLS:
- For the necklace only, you'll need two pairs of pliers - at least one should be a chain nose.

INSTRUCTIONS:

Necklace:
1. Cut two strips from your shirt - about 9 inches long and 1 inch wide. Twist them between your fingers to curl the edges in.
2. Attach a ribbon end or cord end to each end of each strip.
3. Attach a jumpring to each of the ends.
4. Connect a small circle component to the two sides of a large one using jumprings (Image A). Connect this on each side to your two t-shirt strips.
5. On the other ends of the t-shirt strips, attach a clasp and some extra jump rings to close the clasp into.

Bracelet:
6. Start with a piece of t-shirt about 3 inches wide. Make the length double the circumference of your wrist.

7. Fold the strip lengthwise until it's as wide as you want it. Make sure raw ends are on the inside of the folds.
8. Use a simple stitch to sew the two short ends together (Image B).
9. Flip your bracelet inside out and flatten it. Place a circular component in the center between the top and bottom layers. Pull the top layer through the circle and line up with the bottom (Image C). Slip your wrist into the center to wear.

a

b

c

FOUR WITH CRAFT BASICS

Central to the theme of this book is looking outside the jewelry-making aisle in the craft store for your inspiration. That doesn't necessarily mean stepping outside the craft store - there is so much inspiration to be had in the other aisles!

And it goes beyond these few supplies that I included here - buttons, chenille stems (pipe cleaners), zippers, and yarn. As you saw, I've used wooden shapes in many pieces in this book, as well as regular craft paints and glitter. You can also try experimenting with embroidery floss (a more delicate alternative to yarn) in some of these projects, fake flowers, pom poms, feathers, and more. Let the materials lead the way and get creative.

I like to purchase craft basics for jewelry making in bulk sampler packs - larger assortments that come with many different colors, even if it's in smaller sizes or quantities.

BUTTONS FOR BEADS

While I stuck with plain colorful buttons, you can create these pieces with different colors, shapes and sizes. Dig into Grandma's spare button jar to get an eclectic look, or hand-pick them in the craft store.

SUPPLIES:
- 10 assorted buttons for the necklace
- 2 matching buttons for the earrings
- FolkArt brushed silver paint
- flat pad ear studs and backs for the earrings.
- embroidery floss and needle for the earrings.
- E6000 glue for the earrings
- 2 small spacer beads for the necklace.
- 2 headpins for the necklace - they should be about two inches long.
- A finished chain for the necklace

TOOLS:
- for the necklace only, you'll need round nose and chain nose pliers.
- scissors

INSTRUCTIONS:

Necklace:
1. Paint the edges of a few of your buttons silver. This is optional, but adds a pretty touch.
2. Thread a spacer bead on the bottom of each headpin. Thread your buttons on the two headpins in a stack (Image A).
3. Make loops at the tops of the two headpins and close them around your chain.

Earrings:
4. Paint part of the buttons for your earrings silver to add a classy touch. Allow to dry.
5. Thread embroidery floss through the buttonhole a few times to add interest (optional). Knot at the back, add a touch of glue to seal the knot and trim (Image B).
6. Glue your ear studs to the back. Allow it to dry completely before wearing.

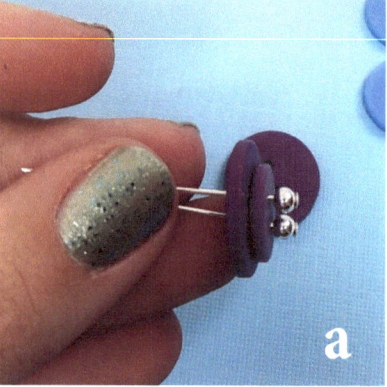

a

b

SKILL — It's becoming familiar: glue something cool to a flat pad ear stud and turn it into an earring! You can apply this in so many ways; just make sure you always glue the earstud towards the top of your embellishment and not in the center when you're working with something big. I like to have about 4mm empty above the part that goes into the ear (Image B) but your preference may be different.

ZIPPER BRACELETS

These simple zipper bracelets have a quirky look to them. If you want it to look classier, go for higher quality metal zippers. Make a few, stack them on your wrists, and wear the zippers open or closed.

SUPPLIES:
- 6 inch zipper
- jumprings
- ribbon crimp ends - make sure they match the width of your zippers
- clasp and connector
- optional: embellishments such as charms, buckle sliders

TOOLS:
- Scissors
- Chain nose pliers

INSTRUCTIONS:
1. Snip off the ends of the zipper right up to the little metal piece that keeps the zipper pull from sliding off (Image A). If you're adding a slider, do it now.
2. Attach the ribbon crimps to the ends.
3. Attach jumprings to the crimps. Attach clasps and connectors to the jumprings.
4. If you're adding charms, attach them to the jumprings now.

SKILL
Just as the previous project showed you how so many things can be turned into studs, this one shows you how to turn practically anything long, narrow, and soft into a bracelet or necklace. Get creative with it!

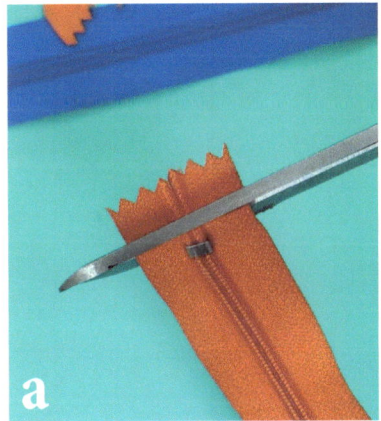

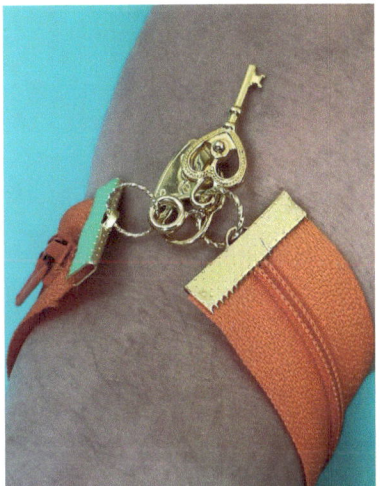

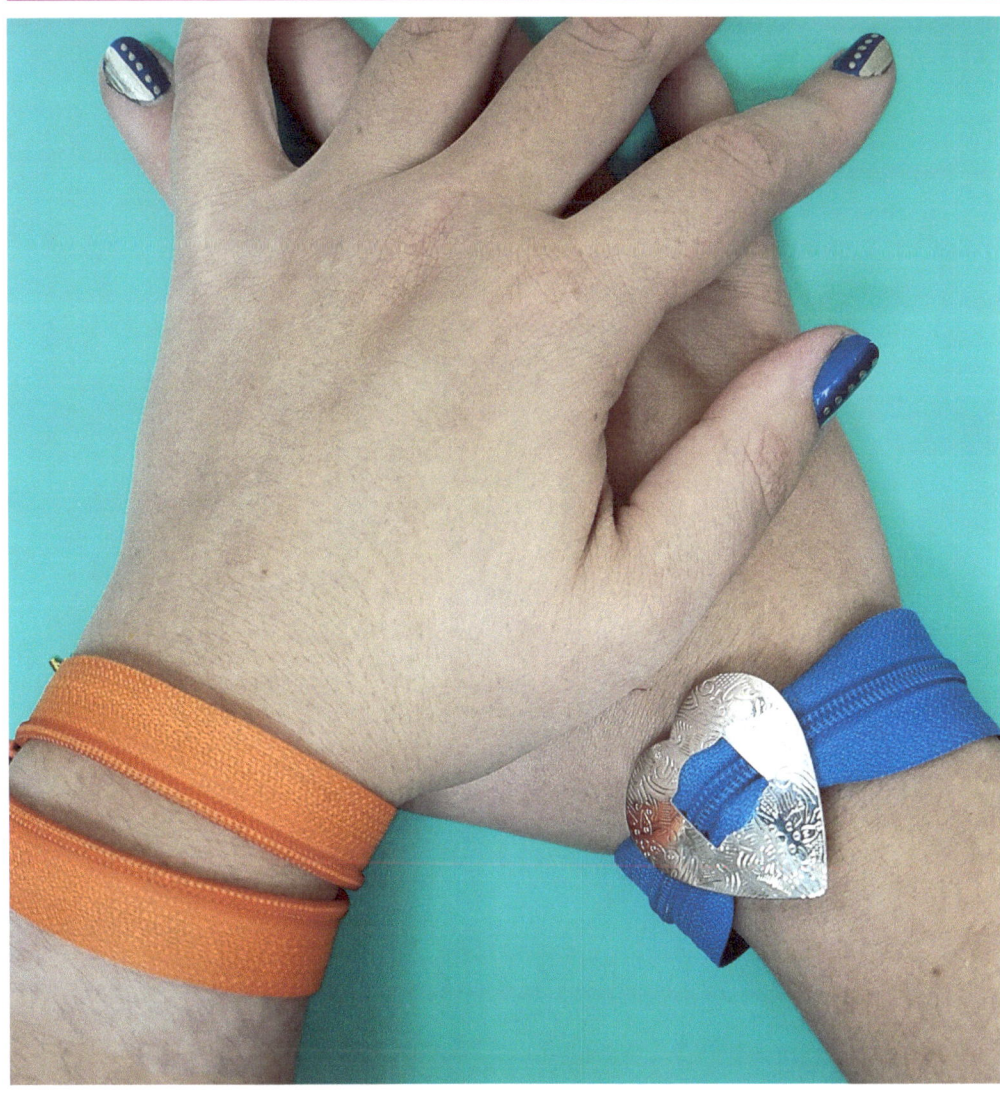

POM POM PIZZAZ

Add life to a plain outfit with pom pom jewlery. Be super bold and wear the pom pom earrings or accessorize with the necklace. With either one, you can tone down the effect by using embroidery floss instead of yarn. The necklace is a lariat necklace which sounds fancy but it's actually really simple. It's a long chain with a pom pom at each end, and it's draped with a loose knot like a scarf might be.

SUPPLIES:
- about 36-40 inches of your favorite chain for the necklace and two inches for the earrings (1 inch for each)
- yarn
- earwires
- 4 jumprings - 2 each for the necklace and earrings

TOOLS:
- 2 pairs of pliers (any)
- wire cutters

INSTRUCTIONS:

Earrings:
1. Wrap yarn around 2 fingers about 20 times. Don't wrap too tight!
2. Tie the entire bundle in the center using another piece of yarn. Gently slip it off your fingers. Double knot it.
3. Snip all the loops open (Image A). Trim your pom pom all around so that it's the size you want it. Make a second matching pom pom.
4. Find the piece of yarn that you added in step 2 - the one that's holding it all together. Slip an open jumpring through it (Image B). Attach about an inch of chain to the jumpring and close it.
5. Attach an earwire to the other end of the chain.

Lariat:
6. Make two pom poms - slightly different sizes and colors add interest here!
7. Add jumprings to your pom poms as you did in step 5.
8. Connect the two jumprings with a length of chain long enough to drape loosely around your neck.

PIPE CLEANER LOVE

Pipe cleaners might be the craft material from your childhood, but wrapped the right way, they can create wonderful chenille creations. I used jumbo size ones for extra fuzz.

SUPPLIES:
- a jumbo pipe cleaner (chenille stem)
- a finished chain

INSTRUCTIONS:
1. Bend the two sides of your pipe cleaner upwards, creasing the center, so that it forms a V.
2. Bend the two sides down without creasing it so that it forms an arch where you bend them. Your pipe cleaners should cross over the original V at about the midway point of this new section (Image A).
3. Take the right side and bend it up and down around the mid-point (Image B). Continue wrapping to the left, "filling in" the heart shape but leaving a small loop empty.
4. Repeat with the left side, wrapping it to the right. This should fill that half completely because you're starting off slightly to the right instead of dead center.
5. Make sure all sharp wire edges are tucked into the chenille.
6. Slide a finished chain through the hole you left in step 3.

MAKE IT YOURS

I shared the idea, now you come up with your own designs! Wrap different shapes. Add a bead to a headpin and form a loop on top to make a bead dangle. Hang it from your pipe cleaner creation. Try painting half with gold fabric paint...

a

b

BE INSPIRED TO THINK DIFFERENTLY

Rethink the way you USED to use these craft materials and techniques. Turn any hobby into jewelry!

4 BEADS GONE AWRY

Beads might seem to be the pillars of jewelry making, but what more can you do with them? The answer: a lot. Mess with them, play with their form, glue them together, melt them (with a grown-up's help), and the possibilities are endless. My favorite beads to use unconventionally are square wooden ones and pony beads. You can get wooden beads in natural tones or in fun colors.

TETRIS EARRINGS

I'll confess: these took a few tries to get right and you might find the same when you try it. But it's worth it. Melting pony beads opens up so many new possibilities - just make sure you have a grown-up to help you. Melted beads are hot! These beads are arranged to resemble tetrominoes - a geometric shape containing four connected squares - made famous by the game Tetris. I like to wear these mismatched.

SUPPLIES:

- 4 small (6mm) pony beads in the same color for each earring.
- flat pad ear studs and backs
- E6000 glue
- an oven or toaster/convection oven that you can see into.
- parchment paper and a baking sheet

INSTRUCTIONS:

1. Cut a piece of parchment so that it lies flat on your baking sheet. Place it in a COOL oven.
2. Arrange your beads in tetrominoes on the baking sheet while it's in the cool oven. The beads of each tetromino should touch each other initially.
3. Bake them at 275° F, watching them the entire time. They'll shrink before they start pooling (Image A) When they're almost ready (Image B), use an oven mitt to carefull remove the baking sheet from the oven. They'll melt a bit more once you've removed them. Allow them to cool completely before touching.
4. When it's cool, remove your Tetris pieces and glue on flat pad earstuds. Allow it to dry completely.

Notes:

There is trial and error to this project and now is the perfect time to become comfortable with experimenting.

The way the beads melt can be unpredictable, which is why you might want to try a few versions of each shape initially so that you have usable ones. The good news is: pony beads are inexpensive, so a bit of "learning" leeway won't cost you much.

You can make these with regular sized pony beads; they'll just be much bigger.

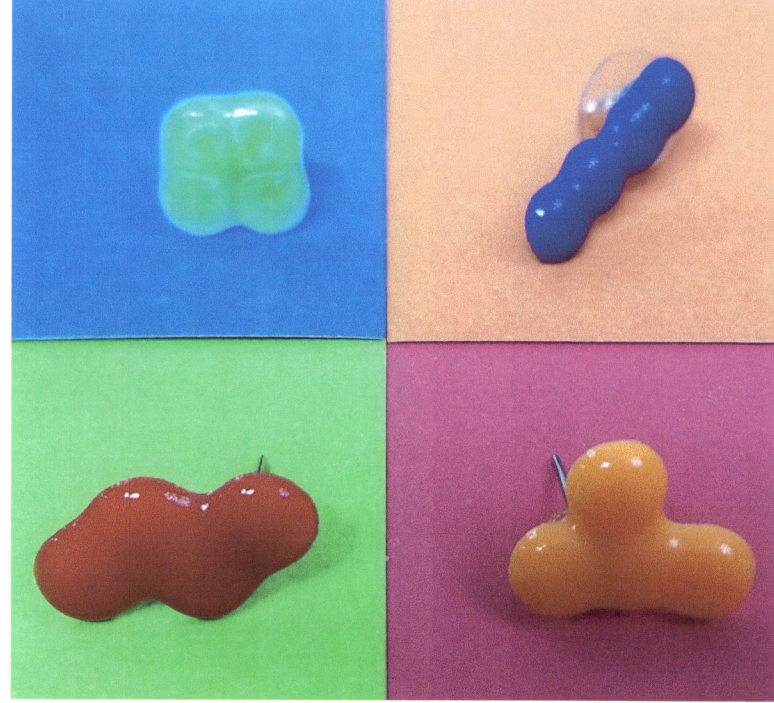

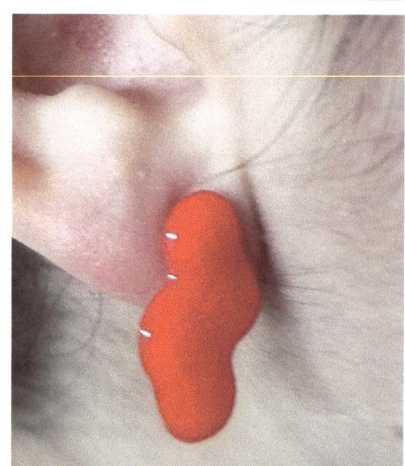

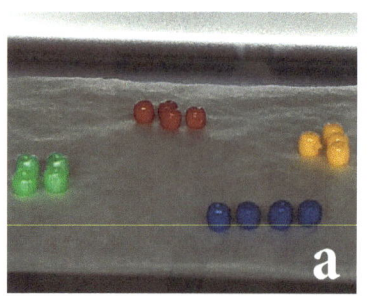
a

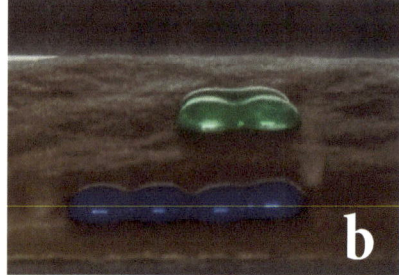
b

FRIENDSHIP BRACELETS

In your head, friendship bracelets might mean knotted embroidery floss. In mine, it means anything you'd give to a friend. Writing on beads is a new way to create something totally custom.

SUPPLIES:
- 3 square wooden beads with large holes
- permanent markers
- twine or string
- glue
- scissors

INSTRUCTIONS:
1. Draw hearts on all four sides of your beads.
2. Thread them onto a piece of twine.
3. Knot your twine on each side of the trio of beads, holding them fixed in the center.
4. Size your bracelet: Tie the left string around the right string, close to the beads, so that it forms a circle that fits your wrist snugly. Make sure that the right string remains straight and is not part of the knot (Image A)
5. Tie the right string around the left close to the beads, so that the two circles of twine align.
6. Tug your knots to make them really secure and make sure they slide nicely. Add a dab of glue to secure the knots, making sure that the knots can still slide. Trim very close to the knots.

SKILL
Tie a sliding knot! Use the skills you learned in this project to make an adustable bracelet using any type of string. The smoother the texture of the string, the more easily it will glide.

a

57

MOSAIC COLLAR

When you have a lot of colorful beads, instead of stringing them, you can glue them to a surface to create a design. This collar, or "bib necklace", works best with different colored beads of the same type.

SUPPLIES:
- felt sheet
- assorted beads
- Tacky Glue
- thick chain
- ribbon (optional)
- clasp and connector

TOOLS:
- any two pliers
- scissors
- detail scissors or a hole punch that will work on felt.

INSTRUCTIONS:
1. Cut a piece of felt to the desired length of the collar portion of your necklace. Punch or cut two holes on the sides of the felt for the chain.
2. Glue on the beads in a pretty pattern. When it's dry, you can trim the base felt to the shape of your pattern (optional).
3. Cut a piece of chain long enough to complete the desired length of your necklace in half. Attach one piece through the hole on each side of the felt portion of your necklace.
4. Attach a clasp to one side and something for the clasp to connect to on the other.
5. If you'd like, tie a ribbon around the base of one portion of chain. Weave it through your chain and knot at the other end. Glue the knots and trim. Repeat with the other portion of chain.

TETRIS JEWELS

Once again inspired by the classic video game, this jewelry set is actually much more subtle - but still has the quirky touch lent by the tetrominoes. It also introduces another way to glue beads.

a

SUPPLIES:

- small square wooden beads
- E6000 or wood glue
- 20 gauge wire or an eyepin
- chain
- a clasp and connector

INSTRUCTIONS:

1. Arrange your beads into assorted tetrominoes/Tetris pieces. Make sure to align the holes so that you create a horizontal hole running through your piece.
2. Glue the beads to each other and allow them to dry completely.
3. Thread a piece of wire horizontally through the aligned holes and form a loop at each end (Image A).
4. Attach a chain of desired length on each end. Attach a clasp and something to connect the clasp to on each end.

MAKE IT YOURS

Try this technique with all differnet shapes and sizes of beads. You can give it a go with colorful beads too. Make flowers, emojis, small and large designs - whatever you'll do it'll have a fun 90's pixelated vibe.

FOUR COOL FRIENDSHIPS

My first experimentation in the world of jewelry making, as with so many kids, was with friendship bracelets. I invented some new designs, but then kind of grew out of them. These projects are inspired by friendship bracelets but are upgraded in some way.

Any time you add metal accents to jewelry, you're adding a more sophisticated touch. You can take any friendship bracelet design and close it off with a cord end and a proper clasp, and you've already aced it.

These projects can move in any direction you want. But I hope, more than anything else, it teaches you how to incorporate new ideas into friendship bracelet making - whether it's trying the stitches on new surfaces, braiding cool materials, or adding metal accents.

WRAP YOUR EARRINGS

The most basic of friendshp bracelets is made up of knots created around a few threads, with alternating colors. Instead of wrapping strings, you can wrap an object to give it a colorful touch! I tried it on an old pair of hoops and a plain metal headband.

SUPPLIES:
- something to wrap
- embroidery floss in three colors
- E6000 glue
- scissors

INSTRUCTIONS:
1. Cut 3 pieces of embroidery floss about two feet long.
2. Glue them next to each other at the beginning of the piece that you're wrapping (Image A). If you can afford the space, you can wrap them around a few times as I did on the headband, otherwise, just try to keep the glued area to a minimum. Allow it to dry completely.
3. Hold two colors flush against the thing you're wrapping. Start knotting one color around the others and the piece you're wrapping (Image B). Knot 10-20 times until you like how long that color is. Let the location of the knot travel around - that's what creates that cool twist.
4. Move on to the next color: just wrap it around the other two and the earring or headband.
5. Continue until you're done and glue your strings in place, Allow to dry completely and trim close to the glue (Image C).

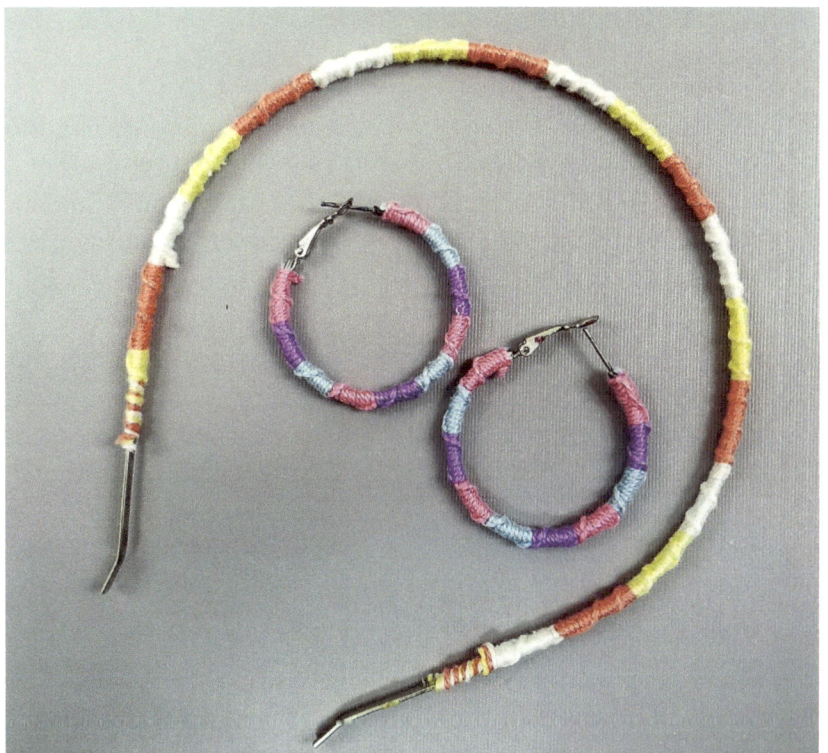

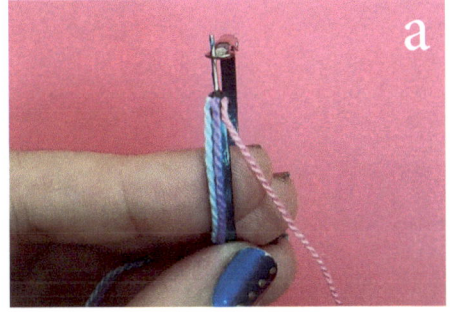
a

b

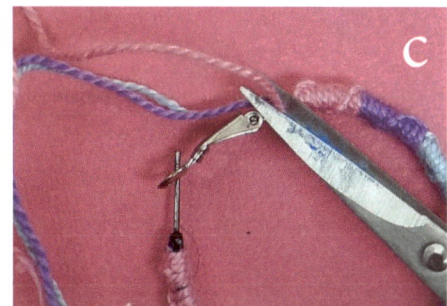
c

KNOT AND LINK

Take the any friendship bracelet design, and update it with some gold or silver plated links or components and you have a beautiful piece. I chose to make the knotted part shorter, and I finished the length of the bracelet with links and jumprings. If you want to skip that, simply cut your strings longer and make the "friendship" part long enough to fit.

SUPPLIES:
- embroidery floss
- large circular component
- ribbon end crimps
- 2 links and 4 jumprings or 6 jumprings
- a clasp and connector

TOOLS:
- 2 pairs of pliers, one should be chain nose
- scissors

INSTRUCTIONS:
1. Cut five one-foot strands each of two different colors of embroidery floss. Line up all the strands of one color and fold in half.
2. Attach to the link by placing the fold of the bundle through the link, then placing the tails through the loop and pulling it tight (Images A-C). Repeat with the second set of strands on the other side of the link.
3. On one side, take your leftmost strand. Tie it around the one immediately to its right twice. Continue tying it twice around each strand, from left to right, until you complete the row. (Image D-E).
4. Take the new leftmost string and repeat step 3, double knotting it around all the other ones, one at a time. Repeat this until you complete 10 rows of knots (Image F).
5. Repeat steps 2-4 on your second color. (Image G).
6. Knot all the strings on each end together, pull very tight and trim about 6mm from the knot. Attach a ribbon crimp (Image H).
7. Increase the length of the bracelet with jumprings and your favorite links and attach a clasp and connector. Try linking and tying in different patterns, using your favorite friendship bracelet designs! (Image I)

BRAIDED BRACELETS

Okay, so now I'm deviating a bit from the knots of friendship bracelets - but that's the point! You can braid almost any stringy material, in this case faux leather, to turn it into a bracelet.

SUPPLIES:
- flat leather cord in three colors
- 2 ribbon end crimps

TOOLS:
- Chain nose pliers

INSTRUCTIONS:
1. Cut 3 pieces of leather cord about double the size you want your bracelet to be.
2. Place them side by side in your ribbon crimp and crimp shut (Image A).
3. Make a braid! Place the left over the cetner, then the right (Image B), repeating till your bracelet is almost long enough.
4. Trim it to size, holding it with your other hand so that the braid doesn't come apart. Add your second ribbon crimp and close it.
5. Cut another piece of leather about 5 inches long and slip it through the holes of the ribbon crimps (Image C).
6. Holding both sides together, tie them in a simple knot. This will become your bracelet closure. If you prefer not to have to open and close a knot each time, you can do this with an elastic, or connect a regular clasp and connector to the ribbon crimps.

MAKE IT YOURS

Braid your fibers - any fibers! - and add "real jewelry" finishes to give it a polished touch. Leather comes in every shape, and size! Try it with colorful leather, add charms, make it with ribbon, baker's twine, or anything you want.

a

b

c

WOVEN CHAINS

These simple woven chain bracelets are an old favorite of mine and a great way to turn pretty cords or ribbons into jewelry. I put them in this section because they are fun to stack and hand out to friends, but they are also a beautiful polished finished piece.

SUPPLIES:
- 6.5-7 inches of thick chain
- a toggle clasp
- leather cord or ribbon
- glue

TOOLS:
- any two pliers
- scissors

INSTRUCTIONS:
1. Attach one half of your toggle to each end of your chain by opening the end links (Image A).
2. Knot your cord or ribbon tightly around the first link in your chain (Image B). Glue the knot and trim.
3. Lay your bracelet flat. Weave your cord through the chain - over and under (Image C). Knot tightly when you're done and glue the knot. Trim.

FYI A toggle clasp includes a bar shaped side and something for it to hook into. They come in so many shpaes and sizes and are fun to use. Of course, you can use a regular clasp for this bracelet (a jumbo sized lobster claw clasp works great) but since it's such a simple piece, a decorative clasp will shine.

a

b

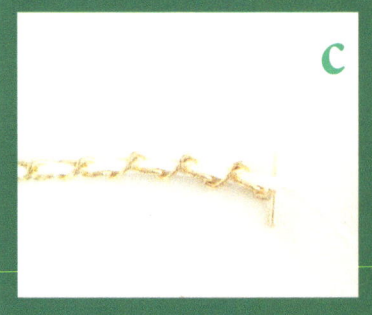

c

4 WITH PAPER

Paper. Yes, I said paper. Successfully creating paper jewelry will depend on one thing: how you finish it. In this chapter I shared a few different ways to finish your paper jewelry. The type of paper you use is important. My favorite is textured cardstock - thick, durable paper with a slightly textured surface. For crafts that are somehow hardened and need a pretty print, I like using Origami paper or.... my own artwork! Using the right Mod Podge when relevant is important as you don't want your finished work to be sticky.

FLOWER STUDS

Made from textured cardstock, these beautiful paper flower studs have a leather-like look. Use any paper flower tutorial and make it in miniature to create a similar effect.

SUPPLIES:
- card stock in two colors. Look for the type that's colored on both sides if you can.
- pen
- fast-drying glue such as glue stick, super glue (adults only) or hot glue (adults only)
- Mod Podge Super Gloss
- thin paint brush
- flat pad ear studs and backs

TOOLS:
- tweezers
- detail scissors

INSTRUCTIONS:
1. Start by cutting a small pentagon shape for each earring - about 8-10mm across.
2. Cut out 5 petals per earring from the first color, keeping it under 1 centimeter long. Cut out five more petals per earring, slightly smaller in size, in your second color.
3. Gently curl the ends of your petals upward around the top end of your paintbrush. You should have the pieces pictured in Image A.
4. Place small dots of glue on your pentagon piece, and, using a tweezers, gently place your large petals on the base, using it as a guide for your petal placement (Image B). Repeat, gluing the smaller petals inside the larger ones.
5. Cut a strip of paper slightly wider than the height of your curled petals. Cut a fringe along the length, about halfway through (Image C).
6. Use the paint brush handle to bend back your fringe a bit. Coil it up, gluing the un-fringed edge as you go along. Glue shut, and glue it down in the center of your flower.
7. Coat with 1-2 layers of Mod Podge super gloss, using a fine paintbrush to get it between and around the petals. Let it dry completely between layers.
8. Glue a flat pad ear stud to the back and allow it to dry completely before wearing.

a

b

c

ARTWORK BROOCHES

Turn your artwork into pretty buttons and brooches you can wear! I made these from small parts of my favorite coloring pages, but you can also make art special for this.

SUPPLIES:
- Mod Podge Podgeable Glass Domes
- Mod Podge
- mini artwork (don't use art made with marker - it will dissolve.)
- glue-on bar pin backs
- flat brush
- E6000 glue
- pen
- scissors
- optional: colored paper

INSTRUCTIONS:
- Trace the glass domes on your artwork, cut out.
- Apply a thin, even layer of Mod Podge to the flat side of your domes using a flat brush (Image A).
- Place your artwork face down on the Mod Podge.
- Paint another layer of Mod Podge on top. Allow it to dry completely.
- Glue your bar pin onto the flat side, behind your artwork (Image B).
- Variation: cut your artwork into a shape smaller than the size of your dome. Trace a piece of colored paper the shape of your glass dome. Assemble the same way, placing your artwork down first, followed by the colored paper (see the leaf brooch above).

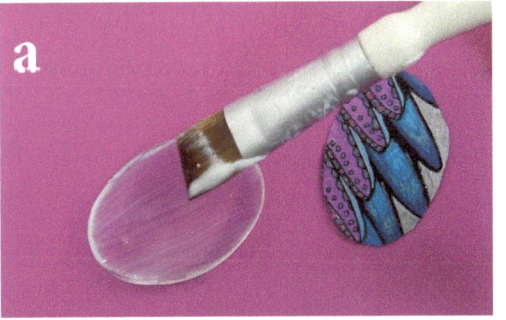

ORIGAMI JEWELRY

Once you get started with origami jewelry, you can create jewelry from any Origami tutorial you find - just make it in mini! Start with a very simple shape: the heart.

SUPPLIES

- origami paper (cut into smaller squares if desired)
- glue
- Mod Podge Super Gloss or Dimensional Magic
- paint brush
- optional- glitter
- flat back pins, jumprings, chains, and other tools and finishes to turn it into jewelry

INSTRUCTIONS:

1. **Make your Origami heart:** Place your paper right side down. Fold from corner to opposite corner and unfold to find center. Fold top corner down to center line (Image A). Fold the bottom corner up to the top fold (Image B). Fold right side up, so that the right half of what was the bottom fold now lines up in the middle (Image C). Repeat with left side. Flip over and fold back any corners you'd like to "round off" your heart (Image D).
2. Glitter up half your heart if you'd like. Allow it to dry comletely.
3. Coat your heart in a layer of Mod Podge Dimensional Magic or Super gloss (Image E). Allow it to dry completely.
4. Turn it into jewelry by either punching a hole and adding a jumpring and chain, or by gluing a pin to the back. Make some super mini and turn them into earrings!

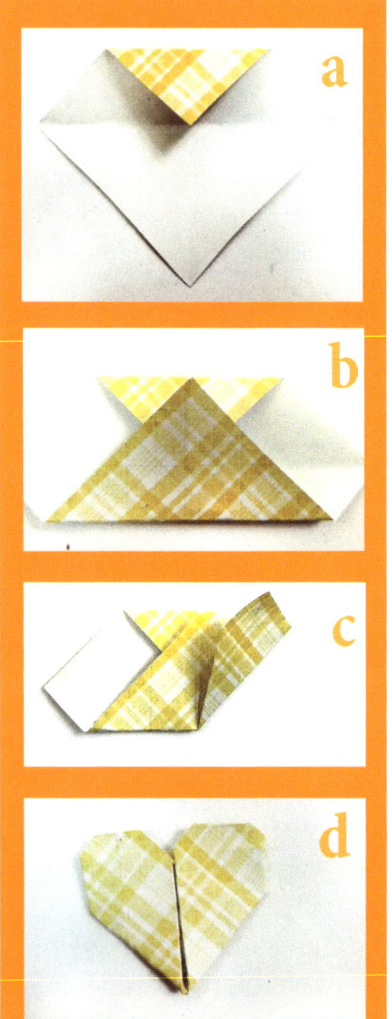

PAPER STUDS

Featherweight earrings are so easy on the ears... and these look like art. I used Mod Podge Dimensional Magic for a durable finish. I angled it so that the leaf part sits on my ear.

SUPPLIES:
- origami paper with small flowers or elements that you like - or draw your own designs!
- Mod Podge Dimensional Magic
- flat pad ear studs and backs
- E6000 glue

TOOLS:
- detail scissors

INSTRUCTIONS:
1. Find two matching (preferably mirror-image) areas on the paper that you'd like to turn into earrings.
2. Gently drip the Dimensional Magic from the bottle to cover that area. Allow it to dry completely.
3. When it's dry, cut out your shapes.
4. Glue on a flat pad ear stud and allow it to dry completely.

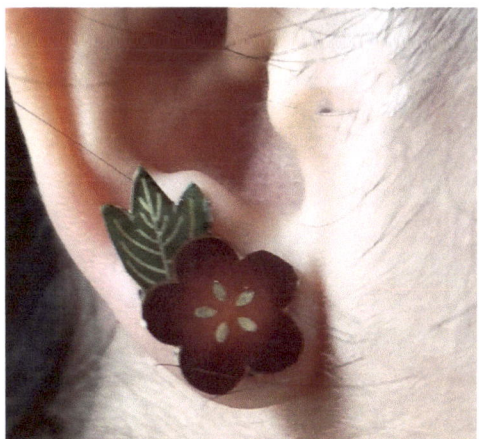

FYI It might be more obvious with a project like this, but you shouldn't wear any jewelry in water! The back of these earrings are unfinished and won't survive being submerged. A bit of rain while you're wearing them won't hurt, though.

SUPPLIES RESOURCES:

Jewelry Making Supplies:

- **FireMountainGems.com** - My favorite spot for stocking up and buying in bulk.
- **Etsy.com** - Find specific items and lots of unique, handmade components from small businesses.
- **Michaels Stores and Michaels.com** - I purchased some of the items for the crafts in this book while browsing Michaels.
- **A.C. Moore Stores** - I love their store brand, Nicole, and used to stock up on simple round toggle clasps when I lived near an A.C. Moore store.
- **Ebay.com** - when it comes to buying small quantities of findings and charms, I like shopping Ebay for low prices and free shipping.
- **Amazon.com** - perfect for medium-size orders, quality control, and very specific items.

Craft Supplies:

- **PlaidOnline.com** - Plaid provided many of the paints, decoupage, brushes, and more for this book. You can find their products in most of the retailers I listed here, but if you want a good summary of each product and its uses, visit the website directly.
- **Michaels Stores and Michaels.com**
- **A.C. Moore Stores**
- **Ebay.com**
- **Amazon.com**
- **Blick Art Materials - dickblick.com** - I absolutely love the prices that Blick has to offer. While it's mainly an art supply store, I've gotten amazing deals on craft materials too, such as leather scraps and paper craft materials.

More Materials Resources:

- List of basic supplies for jewelry making + links - **bit.ly/jewelrysuppliesbeginners**
- List of types of beads and which you need - **bit.ly/beadsforbeginners**
- List of my favorite places to buy jewelry-making supplies online - **bit.ly/jewelryshopsonline**

More Resources for Learning:

- Facebook group for jewelry making inspiration - **bit.ly/fbjewelrygroup**
- Moms & Crafters - **bit.ly/jewelryideas**
- How to Make Jewelry Out of Anything page - **bit.ly/jewelryanything**
- Teach yourself how to make jewelry - **bit.ly/learnjewelry**
- Recommended jewelry making books - **bit.ly/jewelrybooksbeginners**

Visit this resource page online for direct links --> bit.ly/jewelryresource

Or, scan the QR code below with a QR code reading app to be taken directly there!

Additional learning resources, videos, printable templates, and more are available at craftwithanything.com. These will help you create these projects more easily!

INDEX

bangles 30
air dry clay 26, 43
artwork brooches 67
bails, pendant 19
beads 11, 21, 55-59
bottle cap photos 47
bracelets 20, 21, 31, 32, 46, 48, 51, 57, 59, 62, 63, 64
braided bracelets 63
brooches 67, 68
brushed metal 34
buttons 50
chalk 14, 36
charms 11, 25, 31
clasps, closing 18
clay 14, 26, 43
clay pendants 26
collars 58
color blocked studs 29
concrete metallic 37
cord ends 20
cork necklaces 45
craft basics 49-53
crimp beads 21
crimps, ribbon 18
cuffs 24
E6000 glue 11
earrings 27, 29, 34, 35, 36, 40, 41, 50, 52, 56, 61, 66, 68, 69
findings 10
finished chain 26
flower studs 66
friendship bracelets 57
friendships 60-64
garbage 44-48
gems, marbled 32
glitter 23-27
glitter blocked cuffs 24
glue 11
gold nugget earrings 40
headbands 61
hearts 53, 57, 68
hoop earrings 30, 61
jeans bracelet 46
knot and link 62

leaf charms 25
loop, simple 16
loop, wrapped 17
marbled gems 32
markers 14
mermaid earrings 41
Mod Podge 13
mosaic collar 58
nail polish 28-32, 46
nature 39-43
necklaces 20, 42, 43, 45, 48, 50, 52, 53, 59, 68
old tee jewelry 48
origami jewelry 68
paint 33-37
paper 65-69
paper studs 69
pendant bails 19
pendants 19, 25, 26, 31, 36, 37, 47
petal earrings 27
photos 47
pins 25, 68
pipe cleaners 53
pom poms 52
ribbon crimps 18
seaside necklaces 43
simple loop 16
sliding knot 57
studs 29, 40, 41, 50, 56, 66, 69
sunglasses charms 31
supplies 10
tetris earrings 56
tetris jewels 59
toggle clasp 64
tools 10
twig necklaces 42
untired bangles 30
watercolor doodles 35
wire gauges 12
wire wrap 42
wood pieces 13
woven chains 64
wrapped loop 17
wrapping 61
zipper bracelets 51

ABOUT THE AUTHOR:

Menucha Citron Ceder

Born crafting and born crazy, Menucha loves, more than anything, to add a creative spin to a classic project. She has always been crafting on a budget, which trained her to think ouside the box. That's how things like nail polish on twig necklaces are born.

Menucha is the busy mother of two adorable little boys and lives in Far Rockaway, New York. Her full time job is running Moms & Crafters - momsandcrafters.com, a popular creative family lifestyle blog.

One of her greatest pleasures (after acting silly with her babies) is to see her projects being enjoyed by others. She loves it when people share their craft ideas in her Facebook group, "The Sisterhood of Crazy Crafters" (yep, that's an actual thing.)

Menucha survives on coffee (see the following page) and her favorite snack is grated cheese. She takes on new hobbies faster than she can hoard her craft supplies, which is what inspired this new book.

Reach Menucha via email at menucha@momsandcrafters.com
Follow her on Instagram @momsandcrafters

MORE BOOKS BY MENUCHA:

Coloring for Coffee Lovers

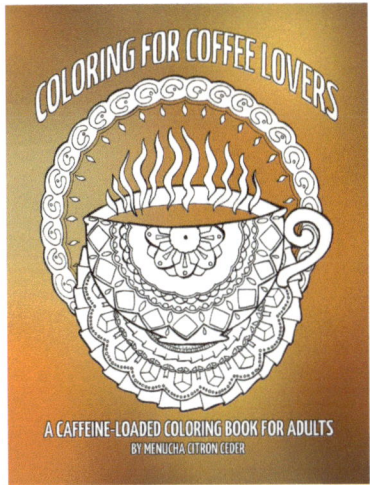

Get your coffee on! With over 25 pages of coffee love to color, this intricately illustrated coloring book will truly help you unwind and relax. Grab that cuppa, grab your colored pencils, and get to it!

Postcards Coloring Book for Creative Adults

Pretty places and favorite spaces make this Postcards coloring book special. Bonus: you get full-sized illustrations PLUS post-card-sized of the same. Bon Voyage!

Color-in Recipe Journal

The family gatherings and the food we eat form childhood memories... and grown-up memeries too! Preserve your favorites in this recipe journal, and color each page with care.

- Purchase these books on Amazon: **bit.ly/menuchacc**
- Get the printable versions of these and more cool coloring pages and printables on Etsy: **momsandcrafters.etsy.com**
- Or shop the ebooks and printables on Gumroad: **gumroad.com/momsandcrafters**

Or scan the QR code below with a QR code reading app to be taken directly to the shop.

www.ingramcontent.com/pod-product-compliance
Lightning Source LLC
Chambersburg PA
CBHW042018150426
43197CB00002B/67